milk and honey

milk and
honey

rupi kaur

Andrews McMeel
PUBLISHING®

Andrews McMeel Publishing
a division of Andrews McMeel Universal
1130 Walnut Street, Kansas City, Missouri 64106

www.andrewsmcmeel.com
www.rupikaur.com

24 25 26 27 28 SDB 82 81 80 79 78

ISBN: 978-1-4494-7425-6

Library of Congress Control Number: 2015946719

Illustrations and cover design by Rupi Kaur

FSC
www.fsc.org
MIX
Paper | Supporting
responsible forestry
FSC® C144853

for
the arms
that hold me

my heart woke me crying last night
how can i help i begged
my heart said
write the book

contents

the
hurting

how is it so easy for you
to be kind to people he asked

milk and honey dripped
from my lips as i answered

cause people have not
been kind to me

the first boy that kissed me
held my shoulders down
like the handlebars of
the first bicycle
he ever rode
i was five

he had the smell of
starvation on his lips
which he picked up from
his father feasting on his mother at 4 a.m.

he was the first boy
to teach me my body was
for giving to those that wanted
that i should feel anything
less than whole

and my god
did i feel as empty
as his mother at 4:25 a.m.

you
have been
taught your legs
are a pit stop for men
that need a place to rest
a vacant body empty enough
for guests but no one
ever comes and is
willing to
stay

it is your blood
in my veins
tell me how i'm
supposed to forget

the therapist places
the doll in front of you
it is the size of girls
your uncles like touching

point to where his hands were

you point to the spot
between its legs the one
he fingered out of you
like a confession

how're you feeling

you pull the lump
in your throat out
with your teeth
and say *fine*
numb really

- midweek sessions

he was supposed to be
the first male love of your life
you still search for him
everywhere

- *father*

you were so afraid
of my voice
i decided to be
afraid of it too

she was a rose
in the hands of those
who had no intention
of keeping her

every time you
tell your daughter
you yell at her
out of love
you teach her to confuse
anger with kindness
which seems like a good idea
till she grows up to
trust men who hurt her
cause they look so much
like you

- to fathers with daughters

i've had sex she said
but i don't know
what making love
feels like

if i knew what
safety looked like
i would have spent
less time falling into
arms that were not

sex takes the consent of two
if one person is lying there not doing anything
cause they are not ready
or not in the mood
or simply don't want to
yet the other is having sex
with their body it's not love
it is rape

the idea that we are
so capable of love
but still choose
to be toxic

there is no bigger illusion in the world
than the idea that a woman will
bring dishonor into a home
if she tries to keep her heart
and her body safe

you pinned
my legs to
the ground
with your feet
and demanded
i stand up

the rape will
tear you
in half

but it
will not
end you

you have sadness
living in places
sadness shouldn't live

a daughter should
not have to
beg her father
for a relationship

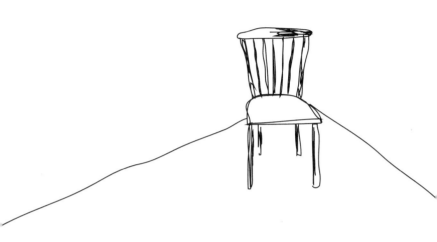

trying to convince myself
i am allowed
to take up space
is like writing with
my left hand
when i was born
to use my right

- the idea of shrinking is hereditary

you tell me to quiet down cause
my opinions make me less beautiful
but i was not made with a fire in my belly
so i could be put out
i was not made with a lightness on my tongue
so i could be easy to swallow
i was made heavy
half blade and half silk
difficult to forget and not easy
for the mind to follow

he guts her
with his fingers
like he's scraping
the inside of a
cantaloupe clean

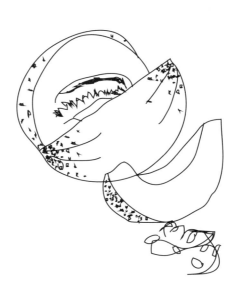

your mother
is in the habit of
offering more love
than you can carry

your father is absent

you are a war
the border between two countries
the collateral damage
the paradox that joins the two
but also splits them apart

emptying out of my mother's belly
was my first act of disappearance
learning to shrink for a family
who likes their daughters invisible
was the second
the art of being empty
is simple
believe them when they say
you are nothing
repeat it to yourself
like a wish
i am nothing
i am nothing
i am nothing
so often
the only reason you know
you're still alive is from the
heaving of your chest

- the art of being empty

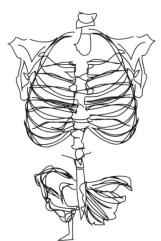

you look just like your mother

       i guess i do carry her tenderness well

you both have the same eyes

       cause we are both exhausted

and the hands

       we share the same wilting fingers

but that rage your mother doesn't wear that anger

       you're right
       this rage is the one thing
       i get from my father

(homage to warsan shire's *inheritance*)

when my mother opens her mouth
to have a conversation at dinner
my father shoves the word hush
between her lips and tells her to
never speak with her mouth full
this is how the women in my family
learned to live with their mouths closed

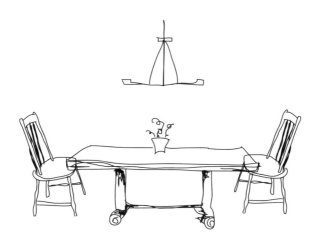

our knees
pried open
by cousins
and uncles
and men
our bodies touched
by all the wrong people
that even in a bed full of safety
we are afraid

father. you always call to say nothing in particular. you
ask what i'm doing or where i am and when the silence
stretches like a lifetime between us i scramble to find
questions to keep the conversation going. what i long to
say most is. i understand this world broke you. it has been
so hard on your feet. i don't blame you for not knowing
how to remain soft with me. sometimes i stay up thinking
of all the places you are hurting which you'll never care
to mention. i come from the same aching blood. from the
same bone so desperate for attention i collapse in on
myself. i am your daughter. i know the small talk is the
only way you know how to tell me you love me. cause it
is the only way i know how to tell you.

you plough into me with two fingers and i am mostly
shocked. it feels like rubber against an open wound.
i do not like it. you begin pushing faster and faster. but i
feel nothing. you search my face for a reaction so i begin
acting like the naked women in the videos you watch when
you think no one's looking. i imitate their moans. hollow
and hungry. you ask if it feels good and i say *yes*
so quickly it sounds rehearsed. but the acting.
you do not notice.

the thing about having
an alcoholic parent
is an alcoholic parent
does not exist

simply
an alcoholic
who could not stay sober
long enough to raise their kids

i can't tell if my mother is
terrified or in love with
my father it all
looks the same

i flinch when you touch me
i fear it is him

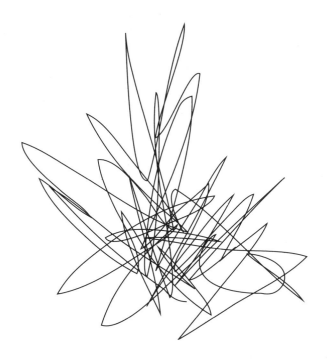

the
loving

when my mother was pregnant
with her second child i was four
i pointed at her swollen belly confused at how
my mother had gotten so big in such little time
my father scooped me in his tree trunk arms and
said the closest thing to god on this earth
is a woman's body it's where life comes from
and to have a grown man tell me something
so powerful at such a young age
changed me to see the entire universe
rested at my mother's feet

i struggle so deeply
to understand
how someone can
pour their entire soul
blood and energy
into someone
without wanting
anything in
return

- *i will have to wait till i'm a mother*

no
it won't
be love at
first sight when
we meet it'll be love
at first remembrance cause
i've seen you in my mother's eyes
when she tells me to marry the type
of man i'd want to raise my son to be like

every revolution
starts and ends
with his lips

what am i to you he asks
i put my hands in his lap
and whisper *you*
are every hope
i've ever had
in human form

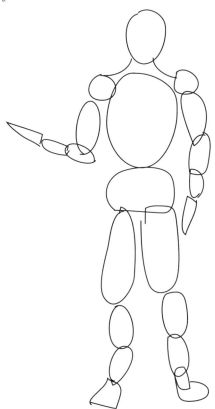

my favorite thing about you is your smell
you smell like
earth
herbs
gardens
a little more
human than the rest of us

i know i
should crumble
for better reasons
but have you seen
that boy he brings
the sun to its
knees every
night

you are the faint line
between faith and
blindly waiting

- *letter to my future lover*

nothing is safer
than the sound of you
reading out loud to me

- *the perfect date*

he placed his hands
on my mind
before reaching
for my waist
my hips
or my lips
he didn't call me
beautiful first
he called me
exquisite

- *how he touches me*

i am learning
how to love him
by loving myself

he says
i am sorry i am not an easy person to want
i look at him surprised
who said i wanted easy
i don't crave easy
i crave goddamn difficult

the very thought of you
has my legs spread apart
like an easel with a canvas
begging for art

i am ready for you
i have always
been
ready for you

- *the first time*

i do not want to have you
to fill the empty parts of me
i want to be full on my own
i want to be so complete
i could light a whole city
and then
i want to have you
cause the two of us combined
could set it on fire

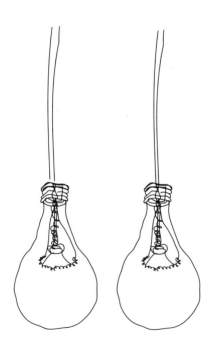

love will come
and when love comes
love will hold you
love will call your name
and you will melt
sometimes though
love will hurt you but
love will never mean to
love will play no games
cause love knows life
has been hard enough already

i'd be lying if i said
you make me speechless
the truth is you make my
tongue so weak it forgets
what language to speak in

he asks me what i do
i tell him i work for a small company
that makes packaging for—
he stops me midsentence
no not what you do to pay the bills
what drives you crazy
what keeps you up at night

i tell him *i write*
he asks me to show him something
i take the tips of my fingers
place them inside his forearm
and graze them down his wrist
goose bumps rise to the surface
i see his mouth clench
muscles tighten
his eyes pore into mine
as though i'm the reason
for making them blink
i break gaze just as
he inches toward me
i step back

so that's what you do
you command attention
my cheeks flush as
i smile shyly
confessing
i can't help it

you might not have been my first love
but you were the love that made
all the other loves
irrelevant

you've touched me
without even
touching me

how do you turn
a forest fire like me
so soft i turn into
running water

you look like you smell of
honey and no pain
let me have a taste of that

your name is
the strongest
positive and negative
connotation in any language
it either lights me up or
leaves me aching for days

you talk too much
he whispers into my ear
i can think of better ways to use that mouth

it's your voice
that undresses me

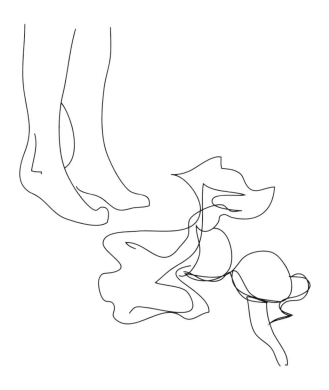

my name sounds so good
french kissing your tongue

you wrap your fingers
around my hair
and pull
this
is how you make
music out of me

- *foreplay*

on days
like this
i need you to
run your fingers
through my hair
and speak softly

- *you*

i want your hands
to hold
not my hands
your lips
to kiss
not my lips
but other places

i need someone
who knows struggle
as well as i do
someone
willing to hold my feet in their lap
on days it is too difficult to stand
the type of person who gives
exactly what i need
before i even know i need it
the type of lover who hears me
even when i do not speak
is the type of understanding
i demand

- the type of lover i need

you move my hand
between my legs
and whisper
make those pretty little fingers dance for me

- solo performance

we've been arguing more than we ought to. about things neither of us remember or care about cause that's how we avoid the bigger questions. instead of asking why we don't say *i love you* to one another as often as we used to. we fight about things like: who was supposed to get up and turn the lights off first. or who was supposed to pop the frozen pizza in the oven after work. taking hits at the most vulnerable parts of one another. we're like fingers on thorns honey. we know exactly where it hurts.

and everything is on the table tonight. like that one time you whispered a name i'm pretty sure wasn't mine in your sleep. or last week when you said you were working late. so i called work but they said you'd already left a couple hours ago. where were you for those couple hours.

i know. i know. your excuses make all the sense in the world. and i get a little carried away for no good reason and eventually begin crying. but what else do you expect baby. i love you so much. i'm sorry i thought you were lying.

that's when you hold your head with your hands in frustration. half begging me to stop. half tired and sick of it. the toxin in our mouths has burnt holes in our cheeks. we look less alive than we used to. less color in our faces. but don't kid yourself. no matter how bad it gets we both know you still wanna nail me to the ground.

especially when i'm screaming so loud our fighting wakes the neighbors. and they come running to the door to save us. baby don't open it.

instead. lie me down. lay me open like a map. and with
your finger trace the places you still want to **** out of
me. kiss me like i am the center point of gravity and you
are falling into me like my soul is the focal point of yours.
and when your mouth is kissing not my mouth
but other places. my legs will split apart out of habit. and
that's when. i pull you in. welcome you. home.

when the entire street is looking out their windows
wondering what all the commotion is. and the fire trucks
come rolling in to save us but they can't distinguish
whether these flames began with our anger or our passion.
i will smile. throw my head back. arch my body like a
mountain you want to split in half. baby lick me.

like your mouth has the gift of reading and i'm your
favorite book. find your favorite page in the soft spot
between my legs and read it carefully. fluently. vividly.
don't you dare leave a single word untouched. and i swear
my ending will be so good. the last few words will come.
running to your mouth. and when you're done. take a
seat. cause it's my turn to make music with my knees
pressed to the ground.

sweet baby. this. is how we pull language out of one
another with the flick of our tongues. this is how we have
the conversation. this. is how we make up.

- *how we make up*

the
breaking

i always
get myself
into this mess
i always let him
tell me i am beautiful
and half believe it
i always jump thinking
he will catch me
at the fall
i am hopelessly
a lover and
a dreamer and
that will be the
death of me

.

when my mother says i deserve better
i snap to your defense out of habit
he still loves me i shout
she looks at me with defeated eyes
the way a parent looks at their child
when they know this is the type of pain
even they can't fix
and says
it means nothing to me if he loves you
if he can't do a single wretched thing about it

you were so distant
i forgot you were there at all

you said. if it is meant to be. fate will bring us back
together. for a second i wonder if you are really
that naive. if you really believe fate works like
that. as if it lives in the sky staring down at us. as
if it has five fingers and spends its time placing us
like pieces of chess. as if it is not the choices we
make. who taught you that. tell me. who
convinced you. you've been given a heart and
a mind that isn't yours to use. that your actions
do not define what will become of you. i want to
scream and shout *it's us you fool. we're the only
ones that can bring us back together.* but
instead i sit quietly. smiling softly through
quivering lips thinking. isn't it such a tragic thing.
when you can see it so clearly but the other person
doesn't.

don't mistake
salt for sugar
if he wants to
be with you
he will
it's that simple

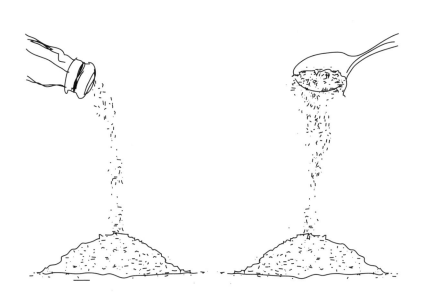

he only whispers *i love you*
as he slips his hands
down the waistband
of your pants

this is where you must
understand the difference
between want and need
you may want that boy
but you certainly
don't need him

you were temptingly beautiful
but stung when i got close

the woman who comes after me will be a bootleg
version of who i am. she will try and write poems
for you to erase the ones i've left memorized on
your lips but her lines could never punch you in
the stomach the way mine did. she will then try to
make love to your body. but she will never
lick, caress, or suck like me. she will be a sad
replacement of the woman you let slip. nothing she
does will excite you and this will break her. when
she is tired of falling apart for a man that doesn't
give back what he takes she will recognize me in
your eyelids staring at her with pity and it'll hit her.
how can she love a man who is busy loving
someone he can never get his hands on again.

the next time you
have your coffee black
you'll taste the bitter
state he left you in
it will make you weep
but you'll never
stop drinking
you'd rather have the
darkest parts of him
than have nothing

more than anything
i want to save you
from myself

you have spent enough nights
with his manhood curled inside your legs
to forget what loneliness feels like

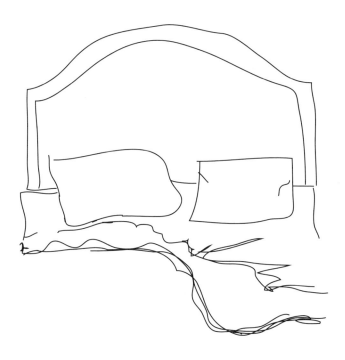

you whisper
i love you
what you mean is
i don't want you to leave

that's the
thing about love
it marinates your lips
till the only word your
mouth remembers
is his name

it must hurt to know
i am your most
beautiful
regret

i didn't leave because
i stopped loving you
i left because the longer
i stayed the less
i loved myself

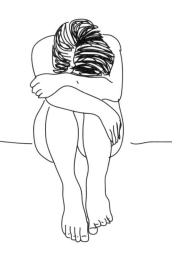

you mustn't have to
make them want you
they must want you themselves

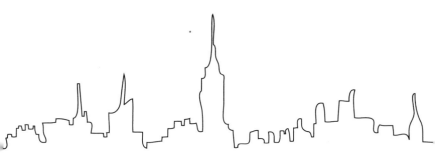

did you think i was a city
big enough for a weekend getaway
i am the town surrounding it
the one you've never heard of
but always pass through
there are no neon lights here
no skyscrapers or statues
but there is thunder
for i make bridges tremble
i am not street meat i am homemade jam
thick enough to cut the sweetest
thing your lips will touch
i am not police sirens
i am the crackle of a fireplace
i'd burn you and you still
couldn't take your eyes off me
cause i'd look so beautiful doing it
you'd blush
i am not a hotel room i am home
i am not the whiskey you want
i am the water you need
don't come here with expectations
and try to make a vacation out of me

the one who arrives after you
will remind me love is
supposed to be soft

he will taste
like the poetry
i wish i could write

if
he can't help but
degrade other women
when they're not looking
if toxicity is central
to his language
he could hold you
in his lap and be soft
honey
that man could feed you sugar and
douse you in rose water
but that still could not
make him sweet

- *if you want to know the type of man he is*

i am a museum full of art
but you had your eyes shut

you must have known
you were wrong
when your fingers
were dipped inside me
searching for honey that
would not come for you

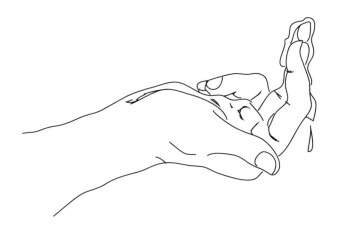

the thing
worth holding on to
would not have let go

when you are broken
and he has left you
do not question
whether you were
enough
the problem was
you were so enough
he was not able to carry it

love made the danger
in you look like safety

even when you undress her
you are searching for me
i am sorry i
taste so good
when the two of you
make love it is
still my name
that rolls off your
tongue accidently

you treat them like they
have a heart like yours
but not everyone can be as
soft and as tender

you don't see the
person they are
you see the person
they have the potential to be

you give and give till
they pull everything out of you
and leave you empty

i had to leave
i was tired of
allowing you to
make me feel
anything less
than whole

you were the most beautiful thing i'd ever felt till
now. and i was convinced you'd remain the most
beautiful thing i'd ever feel. do you know how
limiting that is. to think at such a ripe young age i'd
experienced the most exhilarating person i'd ever
meet. how i'd spend the rest of my life just settling.
to think i'd tasted the rawest form of honey and
everything else would be refined and synthetic. that
nothing beyond this point would add up. that all the
years beyond me could not combine themselves to
be sweeter than you.

- *falsehood*

i don't know what living a balanced life feels like
when i am sad
i don't cry i pour
when i am happy
i don't smile i glow
when i am angry
i don't yell i burn

the good thing about feeling in extremes is
when i love i give them wings
but perhaps that isn't
such a good thing cause
they always tend to leave
and you should see me
when my heart is broken
i don't grieve
i shatter

i came all this way
to give you all these things
but you aren't even looking

the abused
and the
abuser

- i have been both

i am undoing you
from my skin

it wasn't you i was kissing
— don't be mistaken

it was him on my mind
your lips were just convenient

it always comes back to you
boils
circles
itches
its way back to you

.

i was music
but you had your ears cut off

my tongue is sour
from the hunger of
missing you

i will not have you
build me into your life
when
what i want is to
build a life with you

- *the difference*

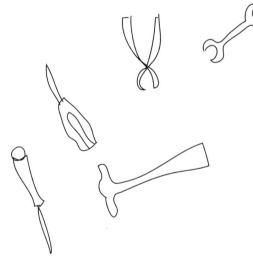

rivers fall from my mouth
tears my eyes can't carry

you are snakeskin
and i keep shedding you somehow
my mind is forgetting
every exquisite detail
of your face
the letting go has
become the forgetting
which is the most
pleasant and saddest thing
to have happened

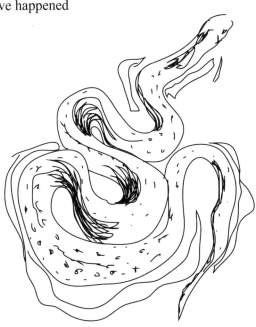

you were not wrong for leaving
you were wrong for coming back
and thinking
you could have me
when it was convenient
and leave when it was not

how can i write
if he took my hands
with him

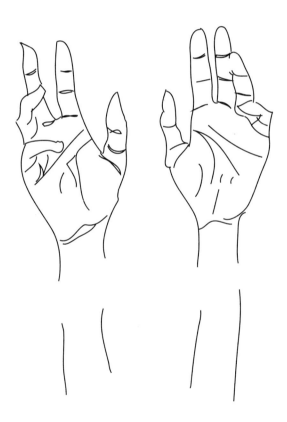

neither of us is happy
but neither of us wants to leave
so we keep breaking one another
and calling it love

we began
with honesty
let us end
in it too

- *us*

your voice
alone
drives me
to tears

i don't know why
i split myself open
for others knowing
sewing myself up
hurts this much
afterward

people go
but how
they left
always stays

love is not cruel
we are cruel
love is not a game
we have made a game
out of love

how can our love die
if it's written
in these pages

even after the hurt
the loss
the pain
the breaking
your body is still
the only one
i want to be
undressed under

the night after you left
i woke up so broken
the only place to put the pieces
were the bags under my eyes

stay
i whispered
as you
shut the door behind you

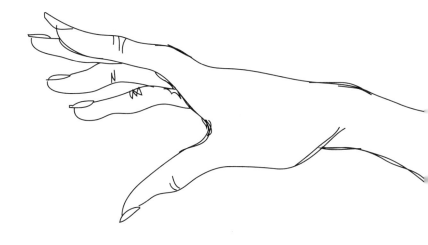

i am confident i am over you. so much that some
mornings i wake up with a smile on my face and
my hands pressed together thanking the universe
for pulling you out of me. thank god i cry. thank
god you left. i would not be the empire i am today
if you had stayed.

but then.

there are some nights i imagine what i might do if
you showed up. how if you walked into the room
this very second every awful thing you've ever
done would be tossed out the closest window and
all the love would rise up again. it would pour
through my eyes as if it never really left in the first
place. as if it's been practicing how to stay silent
so long only so it could be this loud on your arrival.
can someone explain that. how even when the love
leaves. it doesn't leave. how even when i am so
past you. i am so helplessly brought back to you.

he isn't coming back
whispered my head
he has to
sobbed my heart

- wilting

i don't want to be friends
i want all of you

- *more*

i am losing parts of you like i lose eyelashes
unknowingly and everywhere

you cannot leave
and have me too
i cannot exist in
two places at once

- *when you ask if we can still be friends*

i am water

soft enough
to offer life
tough enough
to drown it away

what i miss most is how you loved me. but what i didn't
know was how you loved me had so much to do with
the person i was. it was a reflection of everything i gave
to you. coming back to me. how did i not see that. how.
did i sit here soaking in the idea that no one else would
love me that way. when it was i that taught you. when it
was i that showed you how to fill. the way i needed to be
filled. how cruel i was to myself. giving you credit for my
warmth simply because you had felt it. thinking it was
you who gave me strength. wit. beauty. simply because
you recognized it. as if i was already not these things
before i met you. as if i did not remain all these once you
left.

you leave
but you don't stay gone
why do you do that
why do you
abandon the thing you want to keep
why do you linger
in a place you do not want to stay
why do you think it's okay to do both
go and return all at once

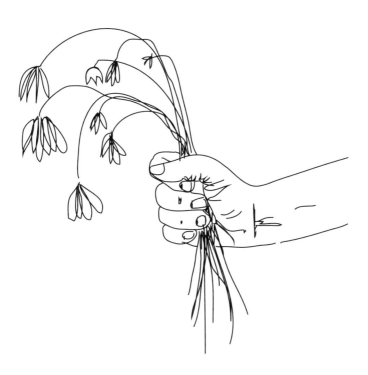

i will tell you about selfish people. even when they know
they will hurt you they walk into your life to taste you
because you are the type of being they don't want to miss
out on. you are too much shine to not be felt. so when they
have gotten a good look at everything you have to offer.
when they have taken your skin your hair your secrets with
them. when they realize how real this is. how much of a
storm you are and it hits them.

that is when the cowardice sets in. that is when the person
you thought they were is replaced by the sad reality of
what they are. that is when they lose every fighting bone in
their body and leave after saying *you will find better than*
me.

you will stand there naked with half of them still hidden
somewhere inside you and sob. asking them why they did
it. why they forced you to love them when they had no
intention of loving you back and they'll say something
along the lines of *i just had to try. i had to give it a chance.*
it was you after all.

but that isn't romantic. it isn't sweet. the idea that they
were so engulfed by your existence they had to risk
breaking it for the sake of knowing they weren't the one
missing out. your existence meant that little next to their
curiosity of you.

that is the thing about selfish people. they
gamble entire beings. entire souls to please their
own. one second they are holding you like the
world in their lap and the next they have
belittled you to a mere picture. a moment.
something of the past. one second. they swallow
you up and whisper they want to spend the rest
of their life with you. but the moment they sense
fear. they are already halfway out the door.
without having the nerve to let you go with
grace. as if the human heart means that little to
them.

and after all this. after all of the taking. the
nerve. isn't it sad and funny how people have
more guts these days to undress you with their
fingers than they do to pick up the phone and
call. apologize. for the loss. and this is how you
lose her.

- *selfish*

to do list (after the breakup):

1. take refuge in your bed.
2. cry. till the tears stop (this will take a few days).
3. don't listen to slow songs.
4. delete their number from your phone even though it is memorized on your fingertips.
5. don't look at old photos.
6. find the closest ice cream shop and treat yourself to two scoops of mint chocolate chip. the mint will calm your heart. you deserve the chocolate.
7. buy new bed sheets.
8. collect all the gifts, t-shirts, and everything with their smell on it and drop it off at a donation center.
9. plan a trip.
10. perfect the art of smiling and nodding when someone brings their name up in conversation.
11. start a new project.
12. whatever you do. do not call.
13. do not beg for what does not want to stay.
14. stop crying at some point.
15. allow yourself to feel foolish for believing you could've built the rest of your life in someone else's stomach.
16. breathe.

rupi kaur

the way they
leave
tells you
everything

143

the
healing

perhaps
i don't deserve
nice things
cause i am paying
for sins i don't
remember

the thing about writing is
i can't tell if it's healing
or destroying me

do not bother holding on to
that thing that does not want you

- *you cannot make it stay*

you must enter a relationship
with yourself
before anyone else

accept that you deserve more
than painful love
life is moving
the healthiest thing
for your heart is
to move with it

it is a part of the
human experience to feel pain
do not be afraid
open yourself to it

- evolving

loneliness is a sign you are in desperate need of yourself

you are in the habit
of co-depending
on people to
make up for what
you think you lack

who tricked you
into believing
another person
was meant to complete you
when the most they can do is complement

do not look for healing
at the feet of those
who broke you

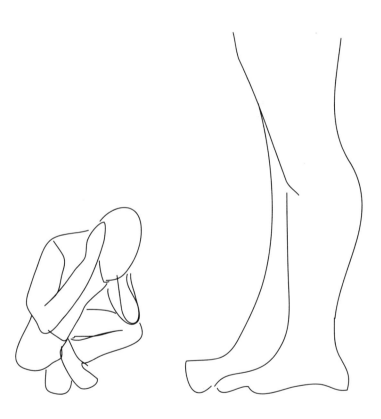

if you were born with
the weakness to fall
you were born with
the strength to rise

perhaps the saddest of all
are those who live waiting
for someone they're not
sure exists

- *7 billion people*

stay strong through your pain
grow flowers from it
you have helped me
grow flowers out of mine so
bloom beautifully
dangerously
loudly
bloom softly
however you need
just bloom

- to the reader

i thank the universe
for taking
everything it has taken
and giving to me
everything it is giving

- *balance*

it takes grace
to remain kind
in cruel situations

fall
in love
with your solitude

there is a difference between
someone telling you
they love you and
them actually
loving you

sometimes
the apology
never comes
when it is wanted

and when it comes
it is neither wanted
nor needed

- *you are too late*

you tell me
i am not like most girls
and learn to kiss me with your eyes closed
something about the phrase—something about
how i have to be unlike the women
i call sisters in order to be wanted
makes me want to spit your tongue out
like i am supposed to be proud you picked me
as if i should be relieved you think
i am better than them

the next time he
points out the
hair on your legs is
growing back remind
that boy your body
is not his home
he is a guest
warn him to
never outstep
his welcome
again

to be
soft
is
to be
powerful

you deserve to be
completely found
in your surroundings
not lost within them

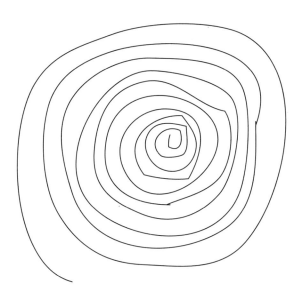

i know it's hard
believe me
i know it feels like
tomorrow will never come
and today will be the most
difficult day to get through
but i swear you will get through
the hurt will pass
as it always does
if you give it time and
let it so let it
go
slowly
like a broken promise
let it go

i like the way the stretch marks
on my thighs look human and
that we're so soft yet
rough and jungle wild
when we need to be
i love that about us
how capable we are of feeling
how unafraid we are of breaking
and tend to our wounds with grace
just being a woman
calling myself
a woman
makes me utterly whole
and complete

my issue with what they consider beautiful
is their concept of beauty
centers around excluding people
i find hair beautiful
when a woman wears it
like a garden on her skin
that is the definition of beauty
big hooked noses
pointing upward to the sky
like they're rising
to the occasion
skin the color of earth
my ancestors planted crops on
to feed a lineage of women with
thighs thick as tree trunks
eyes like almonds
deeply hooded with conviction
the rivers of punjab
flow through my bloodstream so
don't tell me my women
aren't as beautiful
as the ones in
your country

our backs
tell stories
no books have
the spine to
carry

- *women of color*

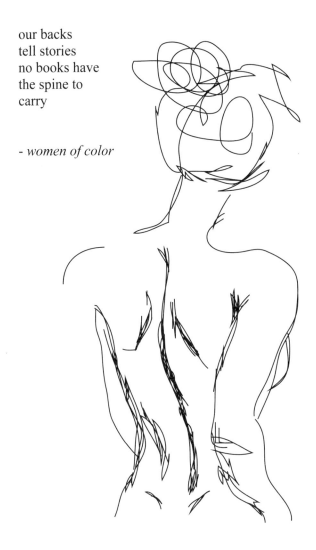

accept yourself
as you were designed

your body
is a museum
of natural disasters
can you grasp how
stunning that is

losing you
was the becoming
of myself

other women's bodies
are not our battlegrounds

removing all the hair
off your body is okay
if that's what you want to do
just as much as keeping all the hair
on your body is okay
if that's what you want to do

- you belong only to yourself

apparently it is ungraceful of me
to mention my period in public
cause the actual biology
of my body is too real

it is okay to sell what's
between a woman's legs
more than it is okay to
mention its inner workings

the recreational use of
this body is seen as
beautiful while
its nature is
seen as ugly

you were a dragon long before
he came around and said
you could fly

you will remain a dragon
long after he's left

i want to apologize to all the women
i have called pretty
before i've called them intelligent or brave
i am sorry i made it sound as though
something as simple as what you're born with
is the most you have to be proud of when your
spirit has crushed mountains
from now on i will say things like
you are resilient or *you are extraordinary*
not because i don't think you're pretty
but because you are so much more than that

i have
what i have
and i am happy

i've lost
what i've lost
and i am
still
happy

- outlook

you look at me and cry
everything hurts

i hold you and whisper
but everything can heal

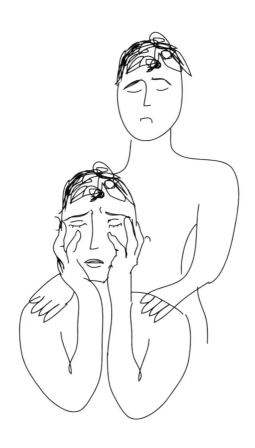

if the hurt comes
so will the happiness

- *be patient*

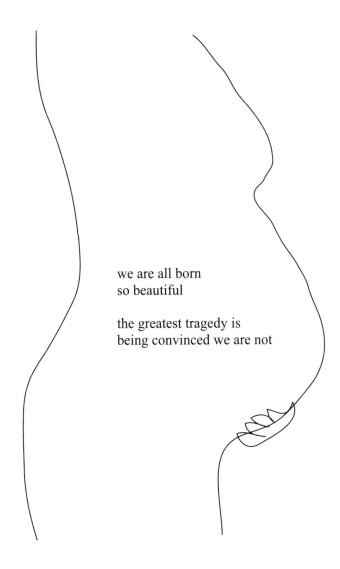

we are all born
so beautiful

the greatest tragedy is
being convinced we are not

the name kaur
makes me a free woman
it removes the shackles that
try to bind me
uplifts me
to remind me i am equal to
any man even though the state
of this world screams to me i am not
that i am my own woman and
i belong wholly to myself
and the universe
it humbles me
calls out and says i have a
universal duty to share with
humanity to nurture
and serve the sisterhood
to raise those that need raising
the name kaur runs in my blood
it was in me before the word itself existed
it is my identity and my liberation

- *kaur*
  a woman of sikhi

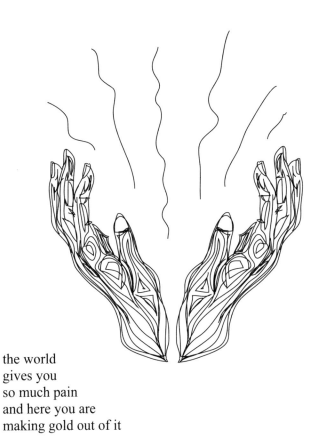

the world
gives you
so much pain
and here you are
making gold out of it

- there is nothing purer than that

how you love yourself is
how you teach others
to love you

my heart aches for sisters more than anything
it aches for women helping women
like flowers ache for spring

the goddess between your legs
makes mouths water

you
are your own
soul mate

some people
are so bitter

to them
you must be kindest

we all move forward when
we recognize how resilient
and striking the women
around us are

for you to see beauty here
does not mean
there is beauty in me
it means there is beauty rooted
so deep within you
you can't help but
see it everywhere

hair
if it was not supposed to be there
would not be growing
on our bodies in the first place

- *we are at war with what comes most naturally to us*

most importantly love
like it's the only thing you know how
at the end of the day all this
means nothing
this page
where you're sitting
your degree
your job
the money
nothing even matters
except love and human connection
who you loved
and how deeply you loved them
how you touched the people around you
and how much you gave them

i want to remain so
rooted to the ground
these tears
these hands
these feet
sink in

- *grounded*

you have to stop
searching for why at some point
you have to leave it alone

if you are not enough for yourself
you will never be enough
for someone else

you must
want to spend
the rest of your life
with yourself
first

of course i want to be successful
but i don't crave success for me
i need to be successful to gain
enough milk and honey
to help those around
me succeed

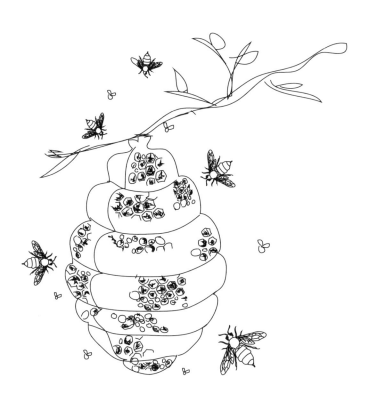

my heartbeat quickens at
the thought of birthing poems
which is why i will never stop
opening myself up to conceive them
the lovemaking
to the words
is so erotic
i am either in love
or in lust with
the writing
or both

what terrifies me most is how we
foam at the mouth with envy
when others succeed
but sigh in relief
when they are failing

our struggle to
celebrate each other is
what's proven most difficult
in being human

your art
is not about how many people
like your work
your art
is about
if your heart likes your work
if your soul likes your work
it's about how honest
you are with yourself
and you
must never
trade honesty
for relatability

- *to all you young poets*

give to those
who have nothing
to give to you

- seva (selfless service)

you split me open
in the most honest
way there is
to split a soul open
and forced me to write
at a time i was sure i
could not write again

- *thank you*

you have made it to the end. with my heart in your hands. thank you. for arriving here safely. for being tender with the most delicate part of me. sit down. breathe. you must be tired. let me kiss your hands. your eyes. they must be wanting of something sweet. i am sending you all my sugar. i would be nowhere and nothing if it were not for you. you've helped me become the woman i wanted to be. but was too afraid to be. do you have any idea how much of a miracle you are. how lovely it's been. and how lovely it will always be. i am kneeling before you. saying thank you. i am sending my love to your eyes. may they always see goodness in people. and may you always practice kindness. may we see each other as one. may we be nothing short of in love with everything the universe has to offer. and may we always stay grounded. rooted. our feet planted firmly onto the earth.

- a love letter from me to you

Rupi Kaur is a poet, artist, and performer.

A breakout literary phenomenon and #1 *New York Times* bestselling author, Rupi Kaur wrote, illustrated, and self-published her first poetry collection, *milk and honey* (2014). Next came its artistic siblings, *the sun and her flowers* (2017) and *home body* (2020), both debuting at #1 on bestseller lists across the world. These collections have sold over 11 million copies and have been translated into over 43 languages, with *milk and honey* surpassing Homer's *Odyssey* as the bestselling poetry of all time. She was also regarded as "writer of the decade" by the *New Republic* and recognized on the *Forbes* 30 under 30 list. In 2022, Kaur released her fourth book, *Healing Through Words*, another bestseller and a journey of guided writing exercises to help readers explore their creativity.

As she has done from the very beginning, Kaur self-produced *Rupi Kaur Live* (2021), the first-of-its-kind poetry special on Amazon Prime Video. Kaur also wrote and narrated an original poem for the short film *Rise* with Reese Witherspoon's media company Hello Sunshine. *Rise* was showcased at the 2023 Sundance Film Festival and is now available on Amazon Prime Video.

Kaur has also graced stages across the globe and completed another sold-out tour in 2023. Her shows are poetic theatrical experiences interlaced with Kaur's own touch of stand-up.

Kaur's work encompasses love, loss, trauma, healing, femininity, and migration. She feels most at home when creating art, performing her poetry onstage, and spending time with family and friends.

milk and honey is a
collection of poetry about
love
loss
trauma
abuse
healing
and femininity
it is split into four chapters
each chapter serves a different purpose
deals with a different pain
heals a different heartache
milk and honey takes readers through
a journey of the most bitter moments in life
and finds sweetness in them
because there is sweetness everywhere
if you are just willing to look

- about the book

the sun
and her flowers

also by rupi kaur

milk and honey

the sun
and her flowers

rupi kaur

Andrews McMeel
PUBLISHING®

Andrews McMeel Publishing
a division of Andrews McMeel Universal
1130 Walnut Street, Kansas City, Missouri 64106

www.andrewsmcmeel.com
www.rupikaur.com

24 25 26 27 28 SDB 22 21 20 19 18

ISBN: 978-1-4494-8679-2

Library of Congress Control Number: 2017948761

Illustrations and design by Rupi Kaur

ATTENTION: SCHOOLS AND BUSINESSES
Andrews McMeel books are available at quantity discounts with bulk purchase
for educational, business, or sales promotional use. For information, please
e-mail the Andrews McMeel Publishing Special Sales Department:
sales@amuniversal.com.

to my makers
kamaljit kaur and suchet singh
i am. because of you.
i hope you look at us
and think
your sacrifices were worth it

to my stunning sisters and brother
prabhdeep kaur
kirandeep kaur
saaheb singh
we are in this together

you define love.

contents

bees came for honey
flowers giggled as they
undressed themselves
for the taking
the sun smiled

- the second birth

wilting

on the last day of love
my heart cracked inside my body

i spent the entire night
casting spells to bring you back

i reached for the last bouquet of flowers
you gave me
now wilting in their vase
one
by
one
i popped their heads off
and ate them

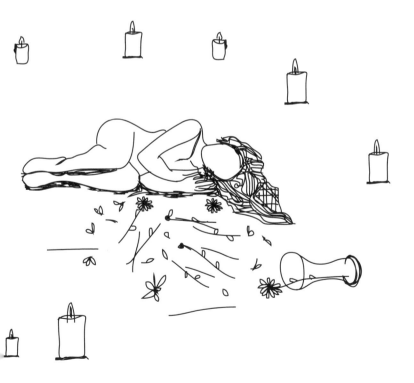

i stuffed a towel at the foot of every door
leave i told the air
i have no use for you
i drew every curtain in the house
go i told the light
no one is coming in
and no one is going out

- *cemetery*

you left
and i wanted you still
yet i deserved someone
who was willing to stay

i spend days in bed debilitated by loss
i attempt to cry you back
but the water is done
and still you have not returned
i pinch my belly till it bleeds
have lost count of the days
sun becomes moon and
moon becomes sun and
i become ghost
a dozen different thoughts
tear through me each second
you must be on your way
perhaps it's best if you're not
i am okay
no
i am angry
yes
i hate you
maybe
i can't move on
i will
i forgive you
i want to rip my hair out
over and over and over again
till my mind exhausts itself into a silence

yesterday
the rain tried to imitate my hands
by running down your body
i ripped the sky apart for allowing it

- jealousy

in order to fall asleep
i have to imagine your body
crooked behind mine
spoon ladled into spoon
till i can hear your breath
i have to recite your name
till you answer and
we have a conversation
only then
can my mind
drift off to sleep

- *pretend*

it isn't what we left behind
that breaks me
it's what we could've built
had we stayed

i can still see our construction hats lying
exactly where we left them
pylons unsure of what to guard
bulldozers gazing out for our return
the planks of wood stiff in their boxes
yearning to be nailed up
but neither of us goes back
to tell them it is over
in time
the bricks will grow tired of waiting and crumble
the cranes will droop their necks in sorrow
the shovels will rust
do you think flowers will grow here
when you and i are off
building something new
with someone else

- *the construction site of our future*

i live for that first second in the morning
when i am still half-conscious
i hear the hummingbirds outside
flirting with the flowers
i hear the flowers giggling
and the bees growing jealous
when i turn over to wake you
it starts all over again
the panting
the wailing
the shock
of realizing
that you've left

- *the first mornings without you*

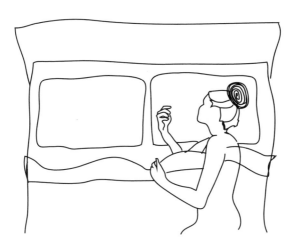

the hummingbirds tell me
you've changed your hair
i tell them i don't care
while listening to them
describe every detail

- *hunger*

i envy the winds
who still witness you

i could be anything
in the world
but i wanted to be his

i tried to leave many times but
as soon as i got away
my lungs buckled under the pressure
panting for air i'd return
perhaps this is why i let you
skin me to the bone
something
was better than nothing
having you touch me
even if it was not kind
was better than not having your hands at all
i could take the abuse
i could not take the absence
i knew i was beating a dead thing
but did it matter
if the thing was dead
when at the very least
i had it

- *addiction*

you break women in like shoes

loving you was breathing
but that breath disappearing
before it filled my lungs

- *when it goes too soon*

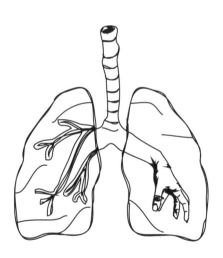

what love looks like

what does love look like the therapist asks
one week after the breakup
and i'm not sure how to answer her question
except for the fact that i thought love
looked so much like you

that's when it hit me
and i realized how naive i had been
to place an idea so beautiful on the image of a person
as if anybody on this entire earth
could encompass all love represented
as if this emotion seven billion people tremble for
would look like a five foot eleven
medium-sized brown-skinned guy
who likes eating frozen pizza for breakfast

what does love look like the therapist asks again
this time interrupting my thoughts midsentence
and at this point i'm about to get up
and walk right out the door
except i paid far too much money for this hour
so instead i take a piercing look at her
the way you look at someone
when you're about to hand it to them
lips pursed tightly preparing to launch into conversation
eyes digging deeply into theirs
searching for all the weak spots

they have hidden somewhere
hair being tucked behind the ears
as if you have to physically prepare for a conversation
on the philosophies or rather disappointments
of what love looks like

well i tell her
i don't think love is him anymore
if love was him
he would be here wouldn't he
if he was the one for me
wouldn't he be the one sitting across from me
if love was him it would have been simple
i don't think love is him anymore i repeat
i think love never was
i think i just wanted something
was ready to give myself to something
i believed was bigger than myself
and when i saw someone
who could probably fit the part
i made it very much my intention
to make him my counterpart

and i lost myself to him
he took and he took
wrapped me in the word *special*
until i was so convinced he had eyes only to see me
hands only to feel me
a body only to be with me
oh how he emptied me

how does that make you feel
interrupts the therapist
well i said
it kind of makes me feel like shit

maybe we're all looking at it wrong
we think it's something to search for out there
something meant to crash into us
on our way out of an elevator
or slip into our chair at a cafe somewhere
appear at the end of an aisle at the bookstore
looking the right amount of sexy and intellectual
but i think love starts *here*
everything else is just desire and projection
of all our wants needs and fantasies
but those externalities could never work out
if we didn't turn inward and learn
how to love ourselves in order to love other people

love does not look like a person
love is our actions
love is giving all we can
even if it's just the bigger slice of cake
love is understanding
we have the power to hurt one another
but we are going to do everything in our power
to make sure we don't
love is figuring out all the kind sweetness we deserve
and when someone shows up

saying they will provide it as you do
but their actions seem to break you
rather than build you
love is knowing whom to choose

you cannot
walk in and out of me
like a revolving door
i have too many miracles
happening inside me
to be your convenient option

- *not your hobby*

you took the sun with you
when you left

i remained committed
long after you were gone
i could not lift my eyes
to meet eyes with someone else
looking felt like betrayal
what excuse would i have
when you came back
and asked where my hands had been

- *loyal*

when you plunged the knife into me
you also began bleeding
my wound became your wound
didn't you know
love is a double-edged knife
you will suffer the way you make me suffer

i think my body knew you would not stay

i long
for you
but you long
for someone else
i deny the one
who wants me
cause i want someone else

- *the human condition*

i wonder if i am
beautiful enough for you
or if i am beautiful at all
i change what i am wearing
five times before i see you
wondering which pair of jeans will make
my body more tempting to undress
tell me
is there anything i can do
to make you think
her
she is so striking
she makes my body forget it has knees
write it in a letter and address it
to all the insecure parts of me
your voice alone drives me to tears
yours telling me i am beautiful
yours telling me i am enough

you're everywhere
except right here
and it hurts

show me a picture
i want to see the face of the woman
who made you forget the one you had at home
what day was it and
what excuse did you feed me
i used to thank the universe
for bringing you to me
did you enter her right as
i asked the almighty
to grant you all you wanted
did you find it in her
did you come crawling out of her
with what you couldn't in me

what draws you to her
tell me what you like
so i can practice

your absence is a missing limb

questions

there is a list of questions
i want to ask but never will
there is a list of questions
i go through in my head
every time i'm alone
and my mind can't stop itself from searching for you
there is a list of questions i want to ask
so if you're listening somewhere
here i am asking them

what do you think happens
to the love that's left behind
when two lovers leave
how blue do you think it gets
before it passes away
does it pass away
or does it still exist somewhere
waiting for us to come back
when we lied to ourselves by
calling this unconditional and left
which one of us hurt more
i shattered into a million little pieces
and those pieces shattered into a million more
crumbled into dust till
there was nothing left of me but the silence

tell me how love
how did the grieving feel for you
how did the mourning hurt

how did you peel your eyes open after every blink
knowing i'd never be there staring back

it must be hard to live with *what ifs*
there must always be this constant dull aching
in the pit of your stomach
trust me
i feel it too
how in the world did we get here
how did we live through it
and how are we still living

how many months did it take
before you stopped thinking of me
or are you still thinking of me
cause if you are
then maybe i am too
thinking of you
thinking of me
with me
in me
around me
everywhere
you and me and us

do you still touch yourself to thoughts of me
do you still imagine my naked naked tiny tiny body
pressed into yours
do you still imagine the curve of my spine and
how you wanted to rip it out of me
cause the way it dipped into my
perfectly rounded bottom
drove you crazy

baby
sugar baby
sweet baby
ever since we left
how many times did you pretend
it was my hand stroking you
how many times did you search for me in your fantasies
and end up crying instead of coming
don't you lie to me
i can tell when you're lying
cause there's always that little bit of
arrogance in your response

are you angry with me
are you okay
and would you tell me if you're not
and if we ever see each other again
do you think you'd reach out and hold me
like you said you would
the last time we spoke and
you talked of the next time we would
or do you think we'd just look
shake in our skin as we pine to
absorb as much as we can of each other
cause by this time we've probably got
someone else waiting at home
we were good together weren't we
and is it wrong that i'm asking you these questions
tell me love
that you have been
looking for these answers too

you call to tell me you miss me
i turn to face the front door of the house
waiting for a knock
days later you call to say you need me
but still aren't here
the dandelions on the lawn
are rolling their eyes in disappointment
the grass has declared you yesterday's news
what do i care
if you love me
or miss me
or need me
when you aren't doing anything about it
if i'm not the love of your life
i'll be the greatest loss instead

where do we go from here my love
when it's over and i'm standing between us
whose side do i run to
when every nerve in my body is pulsing for you
when my mouth waters at the thought
when you are pulling me in just by standing there
how do i turn around and choose myself

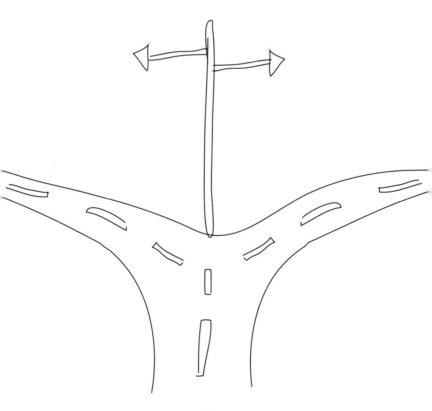

day by day i realize
everything i miss about you
was never there in the first place

- *the person i fell in love with was a mirage*

they leave
and act like it never happened
they come back
and act like they never left

- *ghosts*

i tried to find it
but there was no answer
at the end of the last conversation

- *closure*

you ask
if we can still be friends
i explain how a honeybee
does not dream of kissing
the mouth of a flower
and then settle for its leaves

- i don't need more friends

why is it
that when the story ends
we begin to feel all of it

rise
said the moon
and the new day came
the show must go on said the sun
life does not stop for anybody
it drags you by the legs
whether you want to move forward or not
that is the gift
life will force you to forget how you long for them
your skin will shed till there is not
a single part of you left they've touched
your eyes finally just your eyes
not the eyes which held them
you will make it to the end
of what is only the beginning
go on
open the door to the rest of it

- time

falling

i notice everything i do not have
and decide it is beautiful

i hardened under the last loss. it took something
human out of me. i used to be so deeply emotional i'd
crumble on demand. but now the water has made its
exit. of course i care about the ones around me. i'm just
struggling to show it. a wall is getting in the way. i used
to dream of being so strong nothing could shake me.
now. i am. so strong. that nothing shakes me.
and all i dream is to soften.

- *numbness*

yesterday
when i woke up
the sun fell to the ground and rolled away
flowers beheaded themselves
all that's left alive here is me
and i barely feel like living

- *depression is a shadow living inside me*

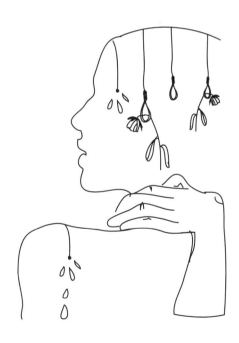

why are you so unkind to me
my body cries

cause you don't look like them
i tell her

you are waiting for someone
who is not coming back
meaning
you are living your life
hoping that someone will realize
they can't live theirs without you

- *realizations don't work like that*

.

a lot of times
we are angry at other people
for not doing what
we should have done for ourselves

- *responsibility*

why
did you leave a door
hanging
open between my legs
were you lazy
did you forget
or did you purposely leave me unfinished

- *conversations with god*

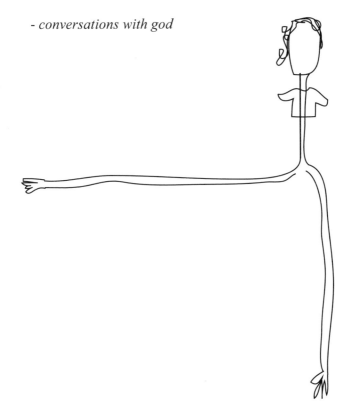

they did not tell me it would hurt like this
no one warned me
about the heartbreak we experience with friends
where are the albums i thought
there were no songs sung for it
i could not find the ballads
or read the books dedicated to writing the grief
we fall into when friends leave
it is the type of heartache that
does not hit you like a tsunami
it is a slow cancer
the kind that does not show up for months
has no visible signs
is an ache here
a headache there
but manageable
cancer or tsunami
it all ends the same
a friend or a lover
a loss is a loss is a loss

- *the underrated heartache*

i hear a thousand kind words about me
and it makes no difference
yet i hear one insult
and all confidence shatters

- *focusing on the negative*

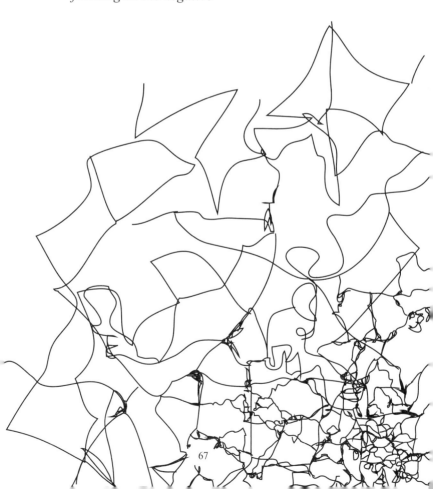

home

it began as a typical thursday from what i recall
sunlight kissed my eyelids good morning
i remember it exactly
climbing out of bed
making coffee to the sound of children playing outside
putting music on
loading the dishwasher
i remember placing flowers in a vase
in the middle of the kitchen table
only when my apartment was spotless
did i step into the bathtub
wash yesterday out of my hair
i decorated myself
like the walls of my home were decorated
with frames bookshelves photos
i hung a necklace around my neck
hooked earrings in
applied lipstick like paint
swept my hair back—just your typical thursday

we ended up at a get-together with friends
at the end you asked if i needed a ride home and
i said *yes* cause our dads worked at the same company
and you'd been to my place for dinner many times

but i should have known
when you began to confuse

kind conversation with flirtation
when you told me to let my hair down
when instead of driving me home
toward the bright intersection
of lights and life—you took a left
to the road that led nowhere
i asked where we were going
you asked if i was afraid
my voice threw itself over the edge of my throat
landed at the bottom of my belly and hid for months
all the different parts in me
turned the lights off
shut the blinds
locked the doors
while i hid at the back of some
upstairs closet of my mind as
someone broke the windows—you
kicked the front door in—you
took everything
and then someone took me
—it was you.

who dove into me with a fork and a knife
eyes glinting with starvation
like you hadn't eaten in weeks
i was a hundred and ten pounds of fresh meat
you skinned and gutted with your fingers
like you were scraping the inside of a cantaloupe clean
as i screamed for my mother
you nailed my wrists to the ground
turned my breasts into bruised fruit

this home is empty now
no gas
no electricity
no running water
the food is rotten
from head to foot i am layered in dust
fruit flies. webs. bugs.
someone call the plumber
my stomach is backed up—i've been vomiting since
call the electrician
my eyes won't light up
call the cleaners to wash me up and hang me to dry

when you broke into my home
it never felt like mine again
i can't even let a lover in without getting sick
i lose sleep after the first date
lose my appetite
become more bone and less skin
forget to breathe
every night my bedroom becomes a psych ward
where panic attacks turn men
into doctors to keep me calm
every lover who touches me—feels like you
their fingers—you
mouths—you
until they're not the ones
on top of me anymore—it's you

and i am so tired
of doing things your way

—it isn't working
i've spent years trying to figure out
how i could have stopped it
but the sun can't stop the storm from coming
the tree can't stop the ax
i can't blame myself for having a hole
the size of your manhood in my chest anymore
it's too heavy to carry your guilt—i'm setting it down
i'm tired of decorating this place with your shame
as if it belongs to me
it's too much to walk around with
what your hands have done
if it's not my hands that have done it

the truth comes to me suddenly—after years of rain
the truth comes like sunlight
pouring through an open window
it takes a long time to get here
but it all comes full circle
it takes a broken person to come searching
for meaning between my legs
it takes a complete. whole. perfectly designed
person to survive it
it takes monsters to steal souls
and fighters to reclaim them
this home is what i came into this world with
was the first home
will be the last home
you can't take it
there is no space for you
no welcome mat

no extra bedrooms
i'm opening all the windows
airing it out
putting flowers in a vase
in the middle of the kitchen table
lighting a candle
loading the dishwasher with all of my thoughts
until they're spotless
scrubbing the countertops
and then
i plan to step into the bathtub
wash yesterday out of my hair
decorate my body in gold
put music on
sit back
put my feet up
and enjoy
this typical thursday afternoon

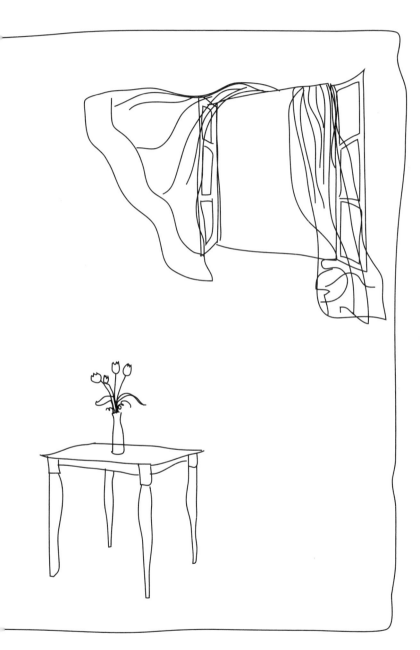

when snow falls
i long for grass
when grass grows
i walk all over it
when leaves change color
i beg for flowers
when flowers bloom
i pick them

- *unappreciative*

tell them i was the
warmest place you knew
and you turned me cold

at home that night
i filled the bathtub with scorching water
tossed in spearmint from the garden
two tablespoons almond oil
some milk
and honey
a pinch of salt
rose petals from the neighbor's lawn
i soaked myself in the mixture
desperate to wash the dirty off
the first hour
i picked pine needles from my hair
counted them one two three
lined them up on their backs
the second hour
i wept
a howling escaped me
who knew girl could become beast
during the third hour
i found bits of him on bits of me
the sweat was not mine
the white between my legs
not mine
the bite marks
not mine
the smell
not mine
the blood
mine
the fourth hour i prayed

it felt like you threw me
so far from myself
i've been trying to find my way back ever since

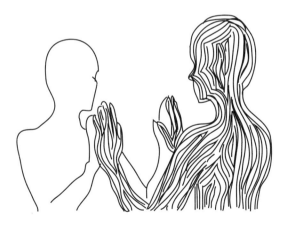

i reduced my body to aesthetics
forgot the work it did to keep me alive
with every beat and breath
declared it a grand failure for not looking like theirs
searched everywhere for a miracle
foolish enough to not realize
i was already living in one

the irony of loneliness
is we all feel it
at the same time

- *together*

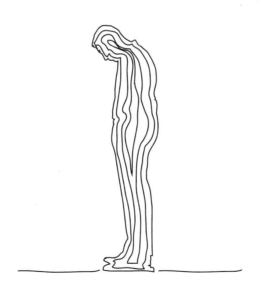

my girlhood was too much hair
thin limbs coated in velvet
it was neighborhood tradition
for the other young girls and i
to frequent basement salons on a weekly basis
run by women in a house
who were my mother's age
had my mother's skin
but looked nothing like my simple mother
they had brown skin with
yellow hair meant for white skin
streaks like zebras
slits for eyebrows
i looked at my own caterpillars with shame
and dreamt mine would be that thin

i sit timidly in the makeshift waiting area
hoping a friend from school would not drop by
a bollywood music video is playing on a tiny
television screen in the corner
someone is getting their legs waxed or hair dyed

when the auntie calls me in
i walk into the room
and make small talk
she leaves for a moment
while i undress my lower half
i slide my pants and underwear off
lie down on the spa bed and wait
when she returns she positions my legs
like an open butterfly
soles of feet together

knees pointing in opposite directions
first the disinfectant wipe
then the cold jelly
how is school and *what are you studying* she asks
turns the laser on
places the head of the machine on my pubic bone
and just like that it begins
the hair follicles around
my clitoris begin burning
with each zap
i wince
shivering with pain

why do i do this
why do i punish my body
for being exactly as it's meant to be
i stop myself halfway through the regret
when i think of him and how
i'm too embarrassed to show him
unless it's clean

i bite down on my lip
and ask if we're almost finished

- *basement aesthetician*

ə

we have been dying
since we got here
and forgot to enjoy the view

- *live fully*

you were mine
and my life was full
you are no longer mine
and my life
is full

my eyes
make mirrors out of
every reflective surface they pass
searching for something beautiful looking back
my ears fish for compliments and praise
but no matter how far they go looking
nothing is enough for me
i go to clinics and department stores
for pretty potions and new techniques
i've tried the lasers
i've tried the facials
i've tried the blades and expensive creams
for a hopeful minute they fill me
make me glow from cheek to cheek
but as soon as i feel beautiful
their magic disappears suddenly
where am i supposed to find it
i am willing to pay any price
for a beauty that makes heads turn
every moment day and night

- *a never-ending search*

this place makes me
the kind of exhausted that has
nothing to do with sleep
and everything to do with
the people around me

- *introvert*

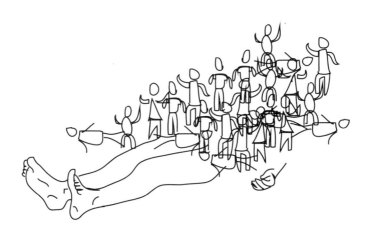

you must see no worth in yourself
if you find me worth less
after you've touched me
as if your hands on my body
magnify you
and reduce me to nothing

- *worth is not something we transfer*

you do not just wake up and become the butterfly

- *growth is a process*

i am having a difficult time right now
comparing myself to other people
i am stretching myself thin trying to be them
making fun of my face like my father
calling it ugly
starving out this premature double chin before it
melts into my shoulders like candle wax
fixing the bags under my eyes that carry the rape
bookmarking surgical procedures for my nose
there is so much that needs tending to
can you point me in the right direction
i want to take this body off
which way back to the womb

like the rainbow
after the rain
joy will reveal itself
after sorrow

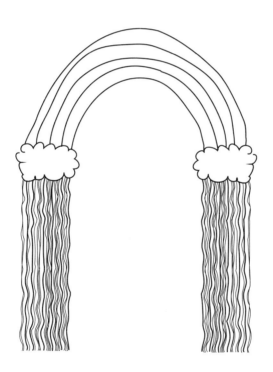

no was a bad word in my home
no was met with the lash
erased from our vocabulary
beaten out of our backs
till we became well-behaved kids
who obediently nodded *yes* to everything
when he climbed on top of me
every part of my body wanted to reject it
but i couldn't say *no* to save my life
when i tried to scream
all that escaped me was silence
i heard *no* pounding her fist
on the roof of my mouth
begging to let her out
but i had not put up the exit sign
never built the emergency staircase
there was no trapdoor for *no* to escape from
i want to ask all the
parents and guardians a question
what use was obedience then
when there were hands
that were not mine inside me

- how can i verbalize consent as an adult if i was
  never taught to as a child

despite knowing
they won't be here for long
they still choose to live
their brightest lives

- *sunflowers*

when you find her
tell her not a day goes by
when i do not think of her
that girl who thinks you are
everything she asked for
when you bounce her off the walls
and she cries
tell her i cry with her too
the sound of drywall crunching into itself
as it's beaten with her head
also lives in my ears
tell her to run to me
i have already unscrewed
my front door off its frame
opened all the windows
inside there is a warm bath running
she does not need your kind of love
i am proof she will get out
and find her way back to herself
if i could survive you
so will she

parts of my body still ache
from the first time they were touched

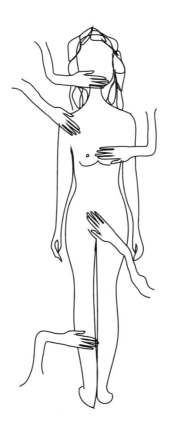

the art of growing

i felt beautiful until the age of twelve
when my body began to ripen like new fruit
and suddenly
the men looked at my newborn hips with salivating lips
the boys didn't want to play tag at recess
they wanted to touch all the new
and unfamiliar parts of me
the parts i didn't know how to wear
didn't know how to carry
and tried to bury in my rib cage

boobs
they said
and i hated that word
hated that i was embarrassed to say it
that even though it was referring to my body
it didn't belong to me
it belonged to them
and they repeated it like
they were meditating upon it
boobs
he said
let me see yours
there is nothing worth seeing here but guilt and shame
i try to rot into the earth below my feet
but i am still standing one foot across
from his hooked fingers
and when he charges to feast on my half moons

i bite into his forearm and decide *i hate this body*
i must have done something terrible to deserve it

when i go home i tell my mother
the men outside are starving
she tells me
i must not dress with my breasts hanging
said *the boys will get hungry if they see fruit*
says i should sit with my legs closed
like a woman oughta
or the men will get angry and fight
said i can avoid all this trouble
if i just learn to act like a lady
but the problem is
that doesn't even make sense
i can't wrap my head around the fact
that i have to convince half the world's population
my body is not their bed
i am busy learning the consequences of womanhood
when i should be learning science and math instead
i like cartwheels and gymnastics so i can't imagine
walking around with my thighs pressed together
like they're hiding a secret
as if the acceptance of my own body parts
will invite thoughts of lust in their heads
i will not subject myself to their ideology
cause slut shaming is rape culture
virgin praising is rape culture
i am not a mannequin in the window
of your favorite shop
you can't dress me up or

throw me out when i am worn
you are not a cannibal
your actions are not my responsibility
you will control yourself

the next time i go to school
and the boys hoot at my backside
i push them down
foot over their necks
and defiantly say
boobs
and the look in their eyes is priceless

when the world comes crashing at your feet
it's okay to let others
help pick up the pieces
if we're present to take part in your happiness
when your circumstances are great
we are more than capable
of sharing your pain

- *community*

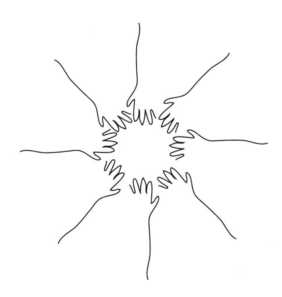

i do not weep
because i'm unhappy
i weep because i have everything
yet i am unhappy

let it go
let it leave
let it happen
nothing
in this world
was promised or
belonged to you anyway

- *all you own is yourself*

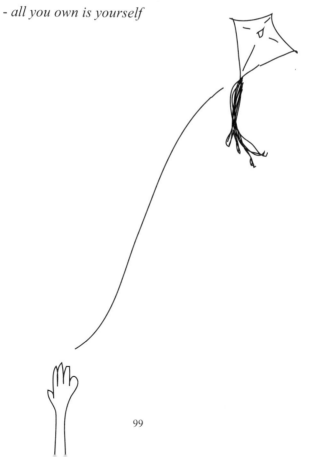

wish pure love and soft peace
upon the ones
who've been unkind to you
and keep moving forward

- *this will free you both*

yes
it is possible
to hate and love someone
at the same time
i do it to myself
every day

somewhere along the way
i lost the self-love
and became my greatest enemy
i thought i'd seen the devil before
in the uncles who touched us as children
the mobs that burned our city to the ground
but i'd never seen someone as hungry
for my flesh as i was
i peeled my skin off just to feel awake
wore it inside out
sprinkled it with salt to punish myself
turmoil clotted my nerves
my blood curdled
i even tried to bury myself alive
but the dirt recoiled
you have already rotted it said
there is nothing left for me to do

- self-hate

the way you speak of yourself
the way you degrade yourself
into smallness
is abuse

- self-harm

when i hit the rock bottom
that exists after the rock bottom
and no rope or hand appeared
i wondered
what if nothing wants me
because i do not want me

- *i am both the poison and the antidote*

first
i went for my words
the *i can't*s. *i won't*s. *i am not good enough*s.
i lined them up and shot them dead
then i went for my thoughts
invisible and everywhere
there was no time to gather them one by one
i had to wash them out
i wove a linen cloth out of my hair
soaked it in a bowl of mint and lemon water
carried it in my mouth as i climbed
up my braid to the back of my head
down on my knees i began to wipe my mind clean
it took twenty-one days
my knees bruised but
i did not care
i was not given the breath
in my lungs to choke it out
i would scrub the self-hate off the bone
till it exposed love

- *self-love*

i have survived far too much to go quietly
let a meteor take me
call the thunder for backup
my death will be grand
the land will crack
the sun will eat itself

- *the day i leave*

i want to honeymoon myself

if i am the longest relationship
of my life
isn't it time to
nurture intimacy
and love
with the person
i lie in bed with each night

- *acceptance*

what is stronger
than the human heart
which shatters over and over
and still lives

i woke up thinking the work was done
i would not have to practice today
how naive to think healing was that easy
when there is no end point
no finish line to cross
healing is everyday work

you have so much
but are always hungry for more
stop looking up at everything you don't have
and look around at everything you do

- *where the satisfaction lives*

you can imitate a light like mine
but you cannot become it

and here you are living
despite it all

this is the recipe of life
said my mother
as she held me in her arms as i wept
think of those flowers you plant
in the garden each year
they will teach you
that people too
must wilt
fall
root
rise
in order to bloom

rooting

they have no idea what it is like
to lose home at the risk of
never finding home again
to have your entire life
split between two lands and
become the bridge between two countries

- *immigrant*

look at what they've done
the earth cried to the moon
they've turned me into one entire bruise

- green and blue

you are an open wound
and we are standing
in a pool of your blood

- *refugee camp*

when it came to listening
my mother taught me silence
if you are drowning their voice with yours
how will you hear them she asked

when it came to speaking
she said *do it with commitment*
every word you say
is your own responsibility

when it came to being
she said *be tender and tough at once*
you need to be vulnerable to live fully
but rough enough to survive it all

when it came to choosing
she asked me to be thankful
for the choices i had that
she never had the privilege of making

- lessons from mumma

leaving her country
was not easy for my mother
i still catch her searching for it
in foreign films
and the international food aisle

i wonder where she hid him. her brother who had
died only a year before. as she sat in a costume of red
silk and gold on her wedding day. she tells me it was
the saddest day of her life. how she had not finished
mourning yet. a year was not enough. there was no way
to grieve that quick. it felt like a blink. a breath. before
the news of his loss had sunk in the decor was already
hung up. the guests had started strolling in. the small
talk. the rush. all mirrored his funeral too much. it felt
as though his body had just been carried away for the
cremation when my father and his family arrived for the
wedding celebrations.

- *amrik singh (1959–1990)*

i am sorry this world
could not keep you safe
may your journey home
be a soft and peaceful one

- rest in peace

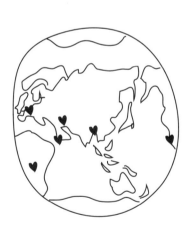

your legs buckle like a tired horse running for safety
drag them by the hips and move faster
you do not have the privilege to rest
in a country that wants to spit you out
you have to keep
going and going
and going
till you reach the water
hand over everything in your name
for a ticket onto the boat
next to a hundred others like you
packed like sardines
you tell the woman beside you
this boat is not strong enough to carry
this much sorrow to a shore
what does it matter she says
if drowning is easier than staying
how many people has this water drunk up
is it all one long cemetery
bodies buried without a country
perhaps the sea is your country
perhaps the boat sinks
because it is the only place that will take you

- boat

what if we get to their doors
and they slam them shut i ask

what are doors she says
when we've escaped the belly of the beast

borders
are man-made
they only divide us physically
don't let them make us
turn on each other

- *we are not enemies*

after the surgery
she tells me
how bizarre it is
that they just took out
the first home of her children

- *hysterectomy february 2016*

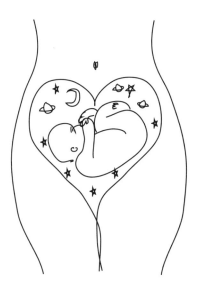

bombs brought entire cities
down to their knees today
refugees boarded boats knowing
their feet may never touch land again
police shot people dead for the color of their skin
last month i visited an orphanage of
abandoned babies left on the curbside like waste
later at the hospital i watched a mother
lose both her child and her mind
somewhere a lover died
how can i refuse to believe
my life is anything short of a miracle
if amidst all this chaos
i was given this life

- *circumstances*

perhaps we are all immigrants
trading one home for another
first we leave the womb for air
then the suburbs for the filthy city
in search of a better life
some of us just happen to leave entire countries

my god
is not waiting inside a church
or sitting above the temple's steps
my god
is the refugee's breath as she's running
is living in the starving child's belly
is the heartbeat of the protest
my god
does not rest between pages
written by holy men
my god
lives between the sweaty thighs
of women's bodies sold for money
was last seen washing the homeless man's feet
my god
is not as unreachable as
they'd like you to think
my god is beating inside us infinitely

advice i would've given
my mother on her wedding day

1. you are allowed to say *no*

2. years ago his father beat the language of love
   out of your husband's back
   he will never know how to say it
   but his actions prove he loves you

3. go with him
   when he enters your body and goes to that place
   sex is not dirty

4. no matter how many times his family brings it up
   do not have the abortion just because i'm a girl
   lock the relatives out and swallow the key
   he will not hate you

5. take your journals and paintings
   across the ocean when you leave
   these will remind you who you are
   when you get lost amid new cities
   they will also remind your children
   you had an entire life before them

6. when your husbands are off
   working at the factories
   make friends with all the other
   lonely women in the apartment complex
   this loneliness will cut a person in half
   you will need each other to stay alive

7. your husband and children will take from your plate
   we will emotionally and mentally starve you
   all of it is wrong
   don't let us convince you that
   sacrificing yourself is
   how you must show love

8. when your mother dies
   fly back for the funeral
   money comes and goes
   a mother is once in a lifetime

9. you are allowed to spend
   a couple dollars on a coffee
   i know there was a time when
   we could not afford it
   but we are okay now. breathe.

10. you can't speak english fluently
    or operate a computer or cell phone
    we did that to you. it is not your fault.
    you are not any less than the
    other mothers with their
    flashy phones and designer clothing
    we confined you to the four walls of this home
    and worked you to the bone
    you have not been your own property for decades

11. there was no rule book for how
    to be the first woman in your lineage
    to raise a family on a strange land by yourself

12. you are the person i look up to most

13. when i am about to shatter
    i think of your strength
    and harden

14. i think you are a magician

15. i want to fill the rest of your life with ease

16. you are the hero of heroes
    the god of gods

in a dream
i saw my mother
with the love of her life
and no children
it was the happiest i'd ever seen her

- *what if*

you split the world
into pieces and
called them countries
declared ownership on
what never belonged to you
and left the rest with nothing

- colonize

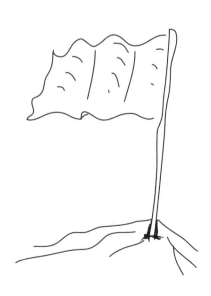

my parents never sat us down in the evenings to share
stories of their younger days. one was always working.
the other too tired. perhaps being an immigrant does
that to you.

the cold terrain of the north engulfed them. their bodies
were hard at work paying in blood and sweat for their
citizenship. perhaps the weight of the new world was
too much. and the pain and sorrow of the old was better
left buried.

i do wish i had unburied it though. i wish i'd pried their
silence apart like a closed envelope. i wish i'd found a
small opening at its very edge. pushed a finger inside
and gently torn it open. they had an entire life before
me which i am a stranger to. it would be my greatest
regret to see them leave this place before i even got to
know them.

my voice
is the offspring
of two countries colliding
what is there to be ashamed of
if english
and my mother tongue
made love
my voice
is her father's words
and mother's accent
what does it matter if
my mouth carries two worlds

- *accent*

for years they were separated by oceans
left with nothing but little photographs of each other
smaller than passport-size photos
hers was tucked into a golden locket
his slipped inside his wallet
at the end of the day
when their worlds went quiet
studying them was their only intimacy

this was a time long before computers
when families in that part of the world
had not seen a telephone or laid their
almond eyes on a colored television screen
long before you and i

as the wheels of the plane touched tarmac
she wondered if this was the place
had she boarded the right flight
should've asked the air hostess twice
like her husband suggested

walking into baggage claim
her heart beat so heavy
she thought it might fall out
eyes darting in every direction
searching for what to do next when
suddenly
right there
in the flesh
he stood
not a mirage—a man
first came relief

then bewilderment
they'd imagined this reunion for years
had rehearsed their lines
but her mouth seemed to forget
she felt a kick in her stomach
when she saw the shadows circling his eyes
and shoulders carrying an invisible weight
it looked like the life had been drained out of him

where was the person she had wed
she wondered
reaching for the golden locket
the one with the photo of the man
her husband did not look like anymore

- *the new world had drained him*

what if
there isn't enough time
to give her what she deserves
do you think
if i begged the sky hard enough
my mother's soul would
return to me as my daughter
so i can give her
the comfort she gave me
my whole life

i want to go back in time and sit beside her. document
her in a home movie so my eyes can spend the rest of
their lives witnessing a miracle. the one whose life
i never think of before mine. i want to know what she
laughed about with friends. in the village within houses
of mud and brick. surrounded by acres of mustard plant
and sugarcane. i want to sit with the teenage version
of my mother. ask about her dreams. become her
pleated braid. the black kohl caressing her eyelids. the
flour neatly packed into her fingertips. a page in her
schoolbooks. even to be a single thread of her cotton
dress would be the greatest gift.

- *to witness a miracle*

1790
he takes the newborn girl from his wife
carries her to the neighboring room
cradles her head with his left hand
and gently snaps her neck with his right

1890
a wet towel to wrap her in
grains of rice and
sand in the nose
a mother shares the trick with her daughter-in-law
i had to do it she says
as did my mother
and her mother before her

1990
a newspaper article reads
a hundred baby girls were found buried
behind a doctor's house in a neighboring village
the wife wonders if that's where he took her
she imagines her daughter becoming the soil
fertilizing the roots that feed this country

1998
oceans away in a toronto basement
a doctor performs an illegal abortion
on an indian woman who already has a daughter
one is burden enough she says

2006
it's easier than you think my aunties tell my mother
they know a family
who've done it three times
they know a clinic. they could get mumma the number.
the doctor even prescribes pills that guarantee a boy.
they worked for the woman down the street they say
now she has three sons

2012
twelve hospitals in the toronto area
refuse to reveal a baby's gender to expecting families
until the thirtieth week of pregnancy
all twelve hospitals are located in areas with high south
asian immigrant populations

- *female infanticide | female feticide*

remember the body
of your community
breathe in the people
who sewed you whole
it is you who became yourself
but those before you
are a part of your fabric

- *honor the roots*

when they buried me alive
i dug my way
out of the ground
with palm and fist
i howled so loud
the earth rose in fear and
the dirt began to levitate
my whole life has been an uprising
one burial after another

- *i will find my way out of you just fine*

my mother sacrificed her dreams
so i could dream

broken english

i think about the way my father
pulled the family out of poverty
without knowing what a vowel was
and my mother raised four children
without being able to construct
a perfect sentence in english
a discombobulated couple
who landed in the new world with hopes
that left the bitter taste of rejection in their mouths
no family
no friends
just man and wife
two university degrees that meant nothing
one mother tongue that was broken now
one swollen belly with a baby inside
a father worrying about jobs and rent
cause no matter what this baby was coming
and they thought to themselves for a split second
was it worth it to put all of our money
into the dream of a country
that is swallowing us whole

papa looks at his woman's eyes
and sees loneliness living where the iris was
wants to give her a home in a country that looks at her
with the word *visitor* wrapped around its tongue
on their wedding day

she left an entire village to be his wife
now she left an entire country to be a warrior
and when the winter came
they had nothing but the heat of their own bodies
to keep the coldness out

like two brackets they faced one another
to hold the dearest parts of them—their children—close
they turned a suitcase full of clothes into a life
and regular paychecks
to make sure the children of immigrants
wouldn't hate them for being the children of immigrants
they worked too hard
you can tell by their hands
their eyes are begging for sleep
but our mouths were begging to be fed
and that is the most artistic thing i have ever seen
it is poetry to these ears
that have never heard what passion sounds like
and my mouth is full of *likes* and *ums* when
i look at their masterpiece
cause there are no words in the english language
that can articulate that kind of beauty
i can't compact their existence into twenty-six letters
and call it a description
i tried once
but the adjectives needed to describe them
don't even exist
so instead i ended up with pages and pages
full of words followed by commas and

more words and more commas
only to realize there are some things
in the world so infinite
they could never use a full stop

so how dare you mock your mother
when she opens her mouth and
broken english spills out
don't be ashamed of the fact that
she split through countries to be here
so you wouldn't have to cross a shoreline
her accent is thick like honey
hold it with your life
it's the only thing she has left of home
don't you stomp on that richness
instead hang it up on the walls of museums
next to dali and van gogh
her life is brilliant and tragic
kiss the side of her tender cheek
she already knows what it feels like
to have an entire nation laugh when she speaks
she is more than our punctuation and language
we might be able to paint pictures and write stories
but she made an entire world for herself

how is that for art

rising

on the first day of love
you wrapped me in the word *special*

you must remember it too
how the rest of the city slept
while we sat awakened for the first time
we hadn't touched yet
but we managed to travel in and out
of each other with our words
our limbs dizzying with enough electricity
to form half a sun
we drank nothing that night
but i was intoxicated
i went home and thought
are we soul mates

i feel apprehensive
cause falling into you
means falling out of him and
i had not prepared for that

- *forward*

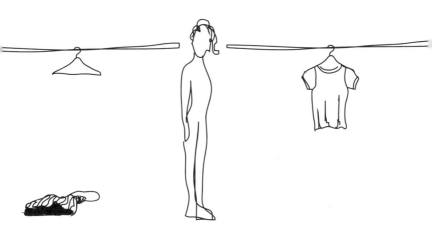

how do i welcome in kindness
when i have only practiced
spreading my legs for the terrifying
what am i to do with you
if my idea of love is violence
but you are sweet
if your concept of passion is eye contact
but mine is rage
how can i call this intimacy
if i crave sharp edges
but your edges aren't even edges
they are soft landings
how do i teach myself
to accept a healthy love
if all i've ever known is pain

i will welcome
a partner
who is my equal

never feel guilty for starting again

the middle place is strange
the part between them and the next
is an awakening from how you saw to
how you will see
this is where their charm wears off
where they are no longer
the god you made them out to be
when the pedestal you carved out of your
bone and teeth no longer serves them
they are unmasked and made mortal again

- the middle place

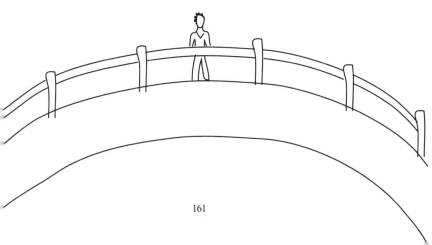

when you start loving someone new
you laugh at the indecisiveness of love
remember when you were sure
the last one was *the one*
and now here you are
redefining *the one* all over again

- *a fresh love is a gift*

i do not need the kind of love
that is draining
i want someone
who energizes me

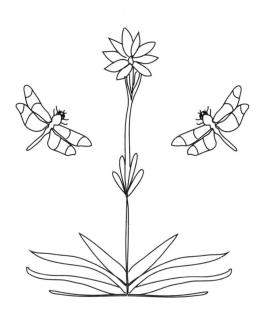

i am trying to not
make you pay for their mistakes
i am trying to teach myself
you are not responsible
for the wound
how can i punish you
for what you have not done
you wear my emotions
like a decorated army vest
you are not cold or
savage or hungry
you are medicinal
you are not them

he makes sure to look right at me
as he places his electric fingers on my skin
how does that feel he asks
commanding my attention
responding is out of the question
i quiver with anticipation
excited and terrified for what's to come
he smiles
knows this is what satisfaction looks like
i am a switchboard
he is the circuits
my hips move with his—rhythmic
my voice isn't my own when i moan—it is music
like fingers on a violin string
he sparks enough electricity within me to power a city
when we finish i look right at him
and tell him
that was magic

when i walked into the coffee shop and saw you. my
body did not react like it had the first time. i waited for
my heart to abandon me. for my legs to freeze up. to fall
to the ground crying at your sight. nothing happened.
there was no connection or movement inside when we
locked eyes. you looked like a regular guy with your
regular clothes and regular coffee. nothing profound
about you. i don't give myself enough credit. my body
must have cleansed itself of you long ago. must have
gotten tired of me behaving like i'd lost the best thing
to have happened. and wrung the insecurities out while
i was busy wallowing in pity. that day i had no makeup
on. my hair was all over the place. i was wearing my
brother's old t-shirt and pajama pants. yet i felt like a
gleaming siren. a mermaid. i did a little dance in the
car while driving home. even though we were both
under the same roof of that coffee shop. i was still solar
systems away from you.

the orange trees refused to blossom
unless we bloomed first
when we met
they wept tangerines
can't you tell
the earth has waited its whole life for this

- *celebration*

why am i always running in circles
between wanting you to want me
and when you want me
deciding it is too emotionally naked
for me to live with
why do i make loving me so difficult
as if you should never have to witness
the ghosts i have tucked under my breast
i used to be more open
when it came to matters like this my love

- *if only we'd met when i was that willing*

i could not contain myself any longer
i ran to the ocean
in the middle of the night
and confessed my love for you to the water
as i finished telling her
the salt in her body became sugar

(ode to sobha singh's *sohni mahiwal)*

i say *maybe this is a mistake. maybe we need more than love to make this work.*

you place your lips on mine. when our faces are buzzing with the ecstasy of kissing you say *tell me that isn't right.* and as much as i'd like to think with my head. my racing heart is all that makes sense. there. right there is the answer you're looking for. in my loss of breath. my lack of words. my silence. my inability to speak means you've filled my stomach with so many butterflies that even if this is a mistake. it could only be right to be this wrong with you.

a
man
who cries

- *a gift*

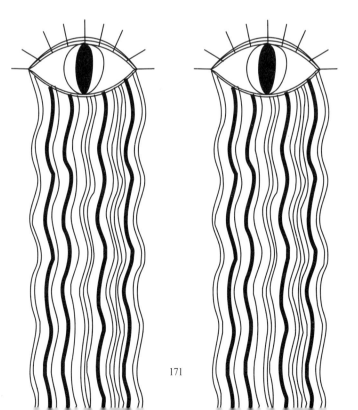

if i'm going to share my life with a partner
it would be foolish not to ask myself
twenty years from now
is this person going to be
someone i still laugh with
or am i just distracted by their charm
do i see us evolving into
new people by the decade
or does the growing ever come to a pause
i don't want to be distracted
by the looks or the money
i want to know if they pull
the best or the worst out of me
deep at the core are our values the same
in thirty years will we still
jump into bed like we're twenty
can i picture us in old age
conquering the world
like we've got young blood
running in our veins

- *checklist*

what is it with you and sunflowers he asks

i point to the field of yellow outside
sunflowers worship the sun i tell him
only when it arrives do they rise
when the sun leaves
they bow their heads in mourning
that is what the sun does to those flowers
it's what you do to me

- the sun and her flowers

sometimes
i stop myself from
saying the words out loud
as if leaving my mouth too often
might wear them down

- *i love you*

the most important conversations
we'll have are with our fingers
when yours nervously graze mine
for the first time during dinner
they'll tighten with fear
when you ask to see me again next week
but as soon as i say yes
they'll stretch out in ease
when they grasp one another
while we're beneath the sheets
the two of us will pretend
we're not weak in the knees
when i get angry
they'll pulse with bitter cries
but when they tremble for forgiveness
you'll see what apologies look like
and when one of us is dying
on a hospital bed at eighty-five
your fingers will grip mine
to say things words can't describe

- *fingers*

this morning
i told the flowers
what i'd do for you
and they blossomed

there is no place
i end and you begin
when your body
is in my body
we are one person

- *sex*

if i had to walk to get to you
it would take eight hundred and twenty-six hours
on bad days i think about it
what i might do if the apocalypse comes
and the planes stop flying
there is so much time to think
so much empty space wanting to be consumed
but no intimacy around to consume it
it feels like being stuck at a train station
waiting and waiting and waiting
for the one with your name on it
when the moon rises on this coast
but the sun still burns shamelessly on yours
i crumble knowing even our skies are different
we have been together so long
but have we really been together if
your touch has not held me long enough
to imprint itself on my skin
i try my hardest to stay present
but without you here
everything at its best
is only mediocre

- *long distance*

i am
made of water
of course i am emotional

they should feel like home
a place that grounds your life
where you go to take the day off

- *the one*

the moon is responsible
for pulling tides
out of still water
darling
i am the still water
and you are the moon

the right one does not
stand in your way
they make space for you
to step forward

when you are
full
and i am
full
we are two suns

your voice does to me
what autumn does to trees
you call to say hello
and my clothes fall naturally

together we are an endless conversation

when death
takes my hand
i will hold you with the other
and promise to find you
in every lifetime

- *commitment*

it was as though
someone had slid ice cubes
down the back of my shirt

- orgasm

you have
been
inside me
before

- *another lifetime*

god must have kneaded you and i
from the same dough
rolled us out as one on the baking sheet
must have suddenly realized
how unfair it was
to put that much magic in one person
and sadly split that dough in two
how else is it that
when i look in the mirror
i am looking at you
when you breathe
my own lungs fill with air
that we just met but we
have known each other our whole lives
if we were not made as one to begin with

- *our souls are mirrors*

to be
two legs
on one body

- *a relationship*

you must have a
honeycomb
for a heart
how else
could a man
be this sweet

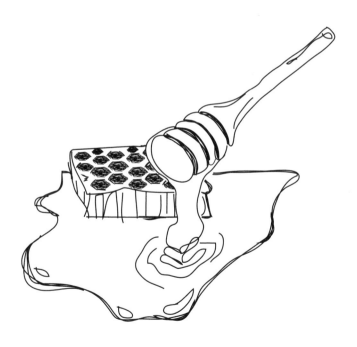

if you got any more beautiful
the sun would leave its place
and come for you

- *the chase*

it has been one of the greatest and most difficult years
of my life. i learned everything is temporary. moments.
feelings. people. flowers. i learned love is about giving.
everything. and letting it hurt. i learned vulnerability
is always the right choice because it is easy to be cold
in a world that makes it so very difficult to remain soft.
i learned all things come in twos. life and death. pain
and joy. salt and sugar. me and you. it is the balance of
the universe. it has been the year of hurting so bad but
living so good. making friends out of strangers. making
strangers out of friends. learning mint chocolate chip
ice cream will fix just about everything. and for the
pains it can't there will always be my mother's arms.
we must learn to focus on warm energy. always. soak
our limbs in it and become better lovers to the world.
for if we can't learn to be kind to each other how will
we ever learn to be kind to the most desperate
parts of ourselves.

blooming

the universe took its time on you
crafted you to offer the world
something different from everyone else
when you doubt
how you were created
you doubt an energy greater than us both

- *irreplaceable*

when the first woman spread her legs
to let the first man in
what did he see
when she led him down the hallway
toward the sacred room
what sat waiting
what shook him so deeply
that all confidence shattered
from then on
the first man
watched the first woman
every night and day
built a cage to keep her in
so she could sin no more
he set fire to her books
called her witch
and shouted whore
until the evening came
when his tired eyes betrayed him
the first woman noticed it
as he unwillingly fell asleep
the quiet humming
the drumming
a knocking between her legs
a doorbell
a voice
a pulse
asking her to open up
and off her hand went running

down the hall
toward the sacred room
she found
god
the magician's wand
the snake's tongue
sitting inside her smiling

- *when the first woman drew magic with her fingers*

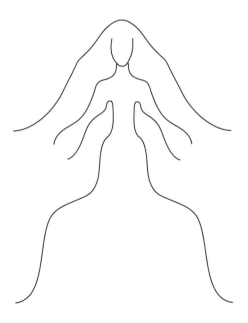

i will no longer
compare my path to others

- i refuse to do a disservice to my life

i am the product of all the ancestors getting together
and deciding these stories need to be told

many tried
but failed to catch me
i am the ghost of ghosts
everywhere and nowhere
i am magic tricks
within magic within magic
none have figured out
i am a world wrapped in worlds
folded in suns and moons
you can try but
you won't get those hands on me

upon my birth
my mother said
there is god in you
can you feel her dancing

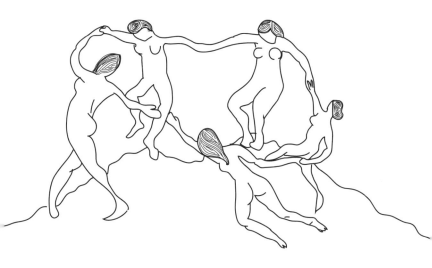

(ode to matisse's *dance)*

as a father of three daughters
it would have been normal
for him to push marriage on us
this has been the narrative for
the women in my culture for hundreds of years
instead he pushed education
knowing it would set us free
in a world that wanted to contain us
he made sure that we learned
to walk independently

there are far too many mouths here
but not enough of them are worth
what you're offering
give yourself to a few
and to those few
give heavily

- *invest in the right people*

i am of the earth
and to the earth i shall return once more
life and death are old friends
and i am the conversation between them
i am their late-night chatter
their laughter and tears
what is there to be afraid of
if i am the gift they give to each other
this place never belonged to me anyway
i have always been theirs

to hate
is an easy lazy thing
but to love
takes strength
everyone has
but not all are
willing to practice

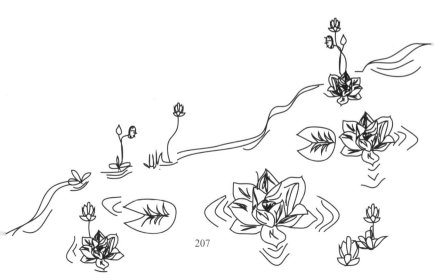

beautiful brown girl
your thick hair is a mink coat not all can afford
beautiful brown girl
you hate the hyperpigmentation
but your skin can't help
carrying as much sun as possible
you are a magnet for the light
unibrow—the bridging of two worlds
vagina—so much darker than the rest of you
cause it is trying to hide a gold mine
you will have dark circles too early
—appreciate the halos
beautiful brown girl
you pull god out of their bellies

look down at your body
whisper
there is no home like you

- thank you

learning to not envy
someone else's blessings
is what grace looks like

i am the first woman in my lineage with freedom of
choice. to craft her future whichever way i choose. say
what is on my mind when i want to. without the whip of
the lash. there are hundreds of firsts i am thankful for.
that my mother and her mother and her mother did not
have the privilege of feeling. what an honor. to be the
first woman in the family who gets to taste her desires.
no wonder i am starving to fill up on this life. i have
generations of bellies to eat for. the grandmothers must
be howling with laughter. huddled around a mud stove
in the afterlife. sipping on steaming glasses of milky
masala chai. how wild it must be for them to see one of
their own living so boldly.

(ode to amrita sher-gil's *village scene 1938)*

trust your body
it reacts to right and wrong
better than your mind does

- *it is speaking to you*

i stand
on the sacrifices
of a million women before me
thinking
what can i do
to make this mountain taller
so the women after me
can see farther

- *legacy*

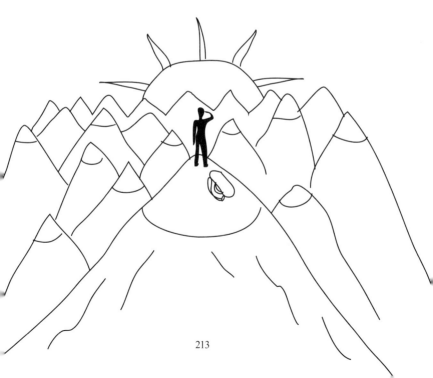

when i go from this place
dress the porch with garlands
as you would for a wedding my dear
pull the people from their homes
and dance in the streets
when death arrives
like a bride at the aisle
send me off in my brightest clothing
serve ice cream with rose petals to our guests
there's no reason to cry my dear
i have waited my whole life
for such a beauty to take
my breath away
when i go
let it be a celebration
for i have been here
i have lived
i have won at this game called life

- *funeral*

it was when i stopped searching for home within others
and lifted the foundations of home within myself
i found there were no roots more intimate
than those between a mind and body
that have decided to be whole

what good am i
if i do not fill the plates
of the ones who fed me
but fill the plates of strangers

- *family*

even if they've been separated
they'll end up together
you can't keep lovers apart
no matter how much
i pluck and pull them
my eyebrows always
find their way
back to each other

- *unibrow*

a child and an elder sat across from each other at a table
a cup of milk and tea before them
the elder asked the child
if she was enjoying her life
the child answered yes
life was good but
she couldn't wait to grow up
and do grown-up things
then the child asked the elder the same question
he too said life was good
but he'd give anything to go back to an age
where moving and dreaming were still possibilities
they both took a sip from their cups
but the child's milk had curdled
the elder's tea had grown bitter
there were tears running from their eyes

the day you have everything
i hope you remember
when you had nothing

she is not a porn category
or the type you look for
on a friday night
she is not needy or easy or weak

- daddy issues is not a punch line

i long to be a lily pad

i made change after change
on the road to perfection
but when i finally felt beautiful enough
their definition of beauty
suddenly changed

what if there is no finish line
and in an attempt to keep up
i lose the gifts i was born with
for a beauty so insecure
it can't commit to itself

- *the lies they sell*

you want to keep
the blood and the milk hidden
as if the womb and breast
never fed you

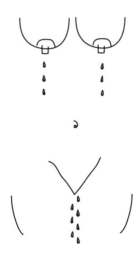

it is a trillion-dollar industry that would collapse
if we believed we were beautiful enough already

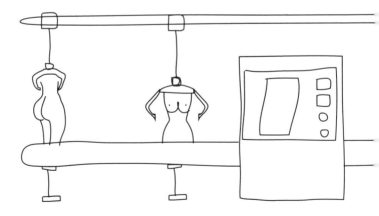

their concept of beauty
is manufactured
i am not

- *human*

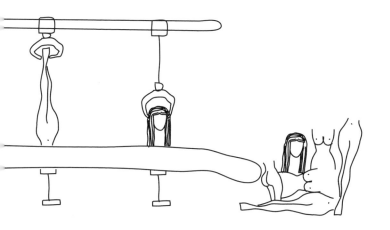

how do i shake this envy
when i see you doing well
sister how do i love myself enough to know
your accomplishments are not my failures

- *we are not each other's competition*

it is a blessing
to be the color of earth
do you know how often
flowers confuse me for home

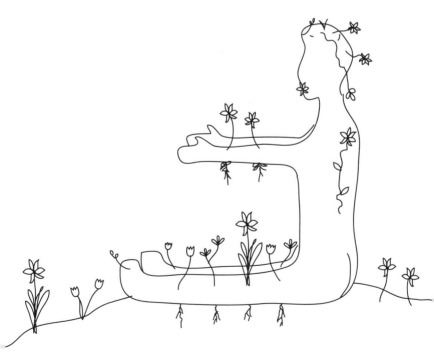

we need more love
not from men
but from ourselves
and each other

- *medicine*

you are a mirror
if you continue to starve yourself of love
you'll only meet people who'll starve you too
if you soak yourself in love
the universe will hand you those
who'll love you too

- *a simple math*

how much
or how little
clothing she has on
has nothing to do with how free she is

- *covered | uncovered*

there are mountains growing
beneath our feet
that cannot be contained
all we've endured
has prepared us for this
bring your hammers and fists
we have a glass ceiling to shatter

- *let's leave this place roofless*

it isn't blood that makes you my sister
it's how you understand my heart
as though you carry it
in your body

what is the greatest lesson a woman should learn

that since day one
she's already had everything she needs within herself
it's the world that convinced her she did not

they convinced me
i only had a few good years left
before i was replaced by a girl younger than me
as though men yield power with age
but women grow into irrelevance
they can keep their lies
for i have just gotten started
i feel as though i just left the womb
my twenties are the warm-up
for what i'm really about to do
wait till you see me in my thirties
now that will be a proper introduction
to the nasty. wild. woman in me.
how can i leave before the party's started
rehearsals begin at forty
i ripen with age
i do not come with an expiration date
and now
for the main event
curtains up at fifty
let's begin the show

- *timeless*

to heal
you have to
get to the root
of the wound
and kiss it all the way up

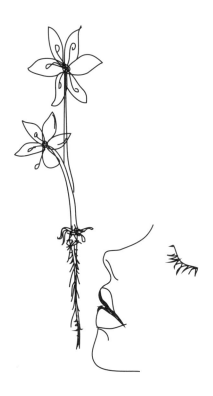

they threw us in a pit to end each other
so they wouldn't have to
starved us of space so long
we had to eat each other up to stay alive
look up look up look up
to catch them looking down at us
how can we compete with each other
when the real monster is too big
to take down alone

when my daughter is living in my belly
i will speak to her like
she's already changed the world
she will walk out of me on a red carpet
fully equipped with the knowledge
that she's capable of
anything she sets her mind to

(ode to raymond douillet's *a short tour and farewell*)

now
is not the time
to be quiet
or make room for you
when we have had no room at all
now
is our time
to be mouthy
get as loud as we need
to be heard

representation
is vital
otherwise the butterfly
surrounded by a group of moths
unable to see itself
will keep trying to become the moth

- representation

take the compliment
do not shy away from
another thing that belongs to you

our work should equip
the next generation of women
to outdo us in every field
this is the legacy we'll leave behind

- *progress*

the road to changing the world
is never-ending

- *pace yourself*

the necessity to protect you overcame me
i love you too much
to remain quiet as you weep
watch me rise to kiss the poison out of you
i will resist the temptation
of my tired feet
and keep marching
with tomorrow in one hand
and a fist in the other
i will carry you to freedom

- love letter to the world

have your eyes ever fallen upon a beast like me
i have the spine of a mulberry tree
the neck of a sunflower
sometimes i am the desert
at times the rain forest
but always the wild
my belly brims over the waistband of my pants
each strand of hair frizzing out like a lifeline
it took a long time to become
such a sweet rebellion
back then i refused to water my roots
till i realized
if i am the only one
who can be the wilderness
then let me be the wilderness
the tree trunk cannot become the branch
the jungle cannot become the garden
so why should i

- it is so full here in myself

many try
but cannot tell the difference
between a marigold and my skin
both of them are an orange sun
blinding the ones who have not learned to love the light

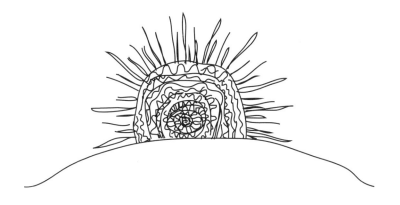

if you have never
stood with the oppressed
there is still time

- *lift them*

the year is done. i spread the past three hundred
sixty-five days before me on the living room carpet.

here is the month i decided to shed everything not
deeply committed to my dreams. the day i refused to be
a victim to the self-pity. here is the week i slept in the
garden. the spring i wrung the self-doubt by its neck.
hung your kindness up. took down the calendar. the
week i danced so hard my heart learned to float above
water again. the summer i unscrewed all the mirrors
from their walls. no longer needed to see myself to feel
seen. combed the weight out of my hair.

i fold the good days up and place them in my back
pocket for safekeeping. draw the match. cremate the
unnecessary. the light of the fire warms my toes.
i pour myself a glass of warm water to cleanse myself
for january. here i go. stronger and wiser into the new.

there is
nothing left
to worry about
the sun and her flowers are here.

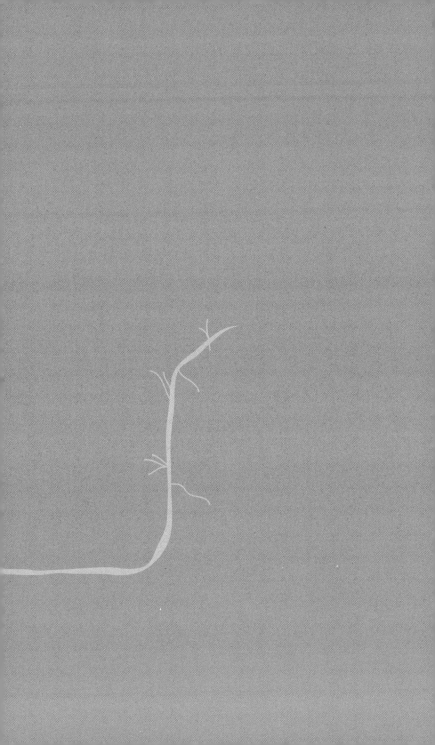

and then there are days when the simple act of breathing leaves you exhausted. it seems easier to give up on this life. the thought of disappearing brings you peace. for so long i was lost in a place where there was no sun. where there grew no flowers. but every once in a while out of the darkness something i loved would emerge and bring me to life again. witnessing a starry sky. the lightness of laughing with old friends. a reader who told me the poems had saved their life. yet there i was struggling to save my own. my darlings. living is difficult. it is difficult for everybody. and it is at that moment when living feels like crawling through a pin-sized hole. that we must resist the urge of succumbing to bad memories. refuse to bow before bad months or bad years. cause our eyes are starving to feast on this world. there are so many turquoise bodies of water left for us to dive in. there is family. blood or chosen. the possibility of falling in love. with people and places. hills high as the moon. valleys that roll into new worlds. and road trips. i find it deeply important to accept that we are not the masters of this place. we are her visitors. and like guests let's enjoy this place like a garden. let us treat it with a gentle hand. so the ones after us can experience it too. let's find our own sun. grow our own flowers. the universe delivered us with the light and the seeds. we might not hear it at times but the music is always on. it just needs to be turned louder. for as long as there is breath in our lungs—we must keep dancing.

Rupi Kaur is a poet, artist, and performer.

A breakout literary phenomenon and #1 *New York Times* bestselling author, Rupi Kaur wrote, illustrated, and self-published her first poetry collection, *milk and honey* (2014). Next came its artistic siblings, *the sun and her flowers* (2017) and *home body* (2020), both debuting at #1 on bestseller lists across the world. These collections have sold over 11 million copies and have been translated into over 43 languages, with *milk and honey* surpassing Homer's *Odyssey* as the bestselling poetry of all time. She was also regarded as "writer of the decade" by the *New Republic* and recognized on the *Forbes* 30 under 30 list. In 2022, Kaur released her fourth book, *Healing Through Words*, another bestseller and a journey of guided writing exercises to help readers explore their creativity.

As she has done from the very beginning, Kaur self-produced *Rupi Kaur Live* (2021), the first-of-its-kind poetry special on Amazon Prime Video. Kaur also wrote and narrated an original poem for the short film *Rise* with Reese Witherspoon's media company Hello Sunshine. *Rise* was showcased at the 2023 Sundance Film Festival and is now available on Amazon Prime Video.

Kaur has also graced stages across the globe and completed another sold-out tour in 2023. Her shows are poetic theatrical experiences interlaced with Kaur's own touch of stand-up.

Kaur's work encompasses love, loss, trauma, healing, femininity, and migration. She feels most at home when creating art, performing her poetry onstage, and spending time with family and friends.

the sun and her flowers is a
collection of poetry about
grief
self-abandonment
honoring one's roots
love
and empowering oneself
it is split into five chapters
wilting. falling. rooting. rising. and blooming.

- about the book

home body

rupi kaur

Andrews McMeel
PUBLISHING®

after feeling disconnected for so long
my mind and body are finally
coming back to each other

- *home body*

contents

mind

i'm in the darkest room of my life

maybe i walked out of the womb with it
is it possible to be born
with such a melancholy spirit
maybe it met me at the airport
slid into my passport
and remained with me
long after we landed in
a country that did not want us
maybe it was on my father's face
when he met us in baggage claim
and i had no idea who he was
maybe the rapist left it behind
or was it that criminal i called a boyfriend
maybe he beat it into me
maybe i met the one
and lost him
maybe it was the love
of my life's parting gift
or maybe
it was all of those things at once

- *where the depression came from*

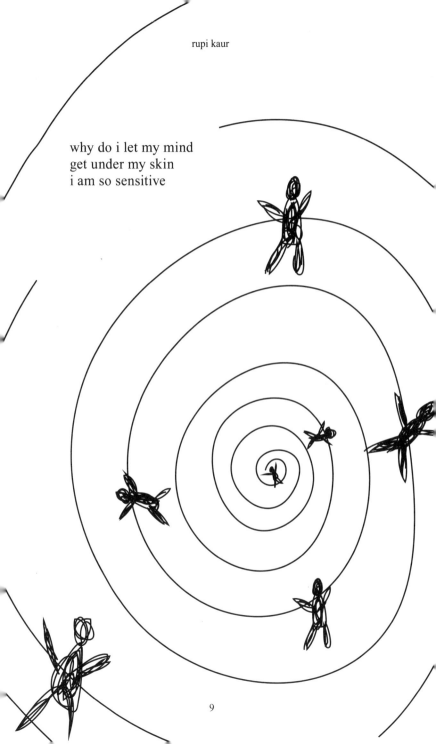

why do i let my mind
get under my skin
i am so sensitive

my mind keeps running off to dark corners
and coming back with reasons for
why i am not enough

sex is a way for people to
transcend into each other
and come apart
a beautiful earthy expression
but for me
sex was my girlhood
dragged to death
he said
we were going to play
then he always locked the door
always chose the game
when i told him to stop
he said i was asking for it
but what did i know
about involuntary orgasms
and agency
and consent
at age 7. 8. 9. and 10.

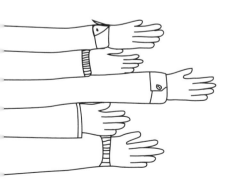

i'll be quiet when
we can say *sexual assault*
and they
stop screaming *liar*

depression is silent
you never hear it coming
and suddenly it's
the loudest voice in your head

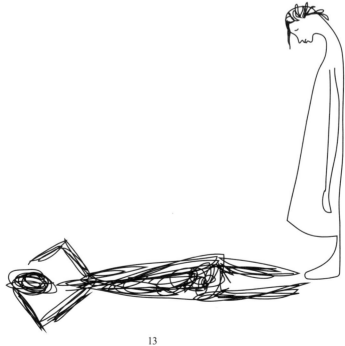

my mind
my body
and i
all live in one place
but it feels like we are
three completely different people

- *disconnected*

while everyone else
was living their life in color
depression froze me in place

nothing lasts forever
let that be the reason you stay
even this sick twisted misery
will not last

- *hope*

i have never known anything more
quietly loud than anxiety

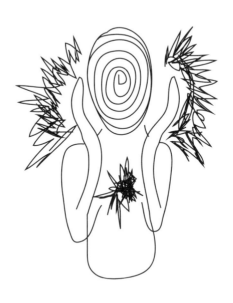

if you could accept
that perfection is impossible
what would you stop obsessing over

you are lonely
but you are not alone

- there is a difference

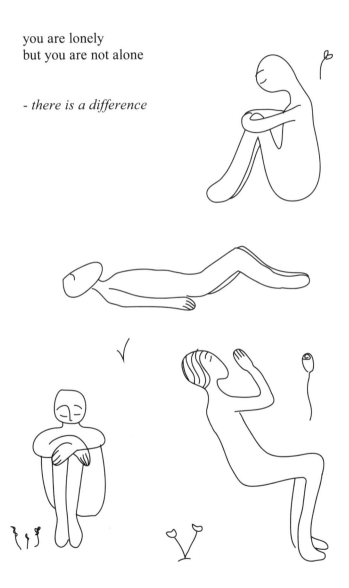

it feels like i'm watching my life happen through
a fuzzy television screen. i feel far away from this
world. almost foreign in this body. as if every happy
memory has been wiped clean from the bowl of my
mind. i close my eyes and i can't remember what
happy feels like. my chest collapses into my stomach
knowing that i have to get up in the morning and
pretend i'm not fading away all over again. i want
to reach out and touch things. i want to feel them
touch me back. i want to live. i want the vitality of
my life back.

abuse doesn't just happen
in romantic relationships
abuse can live
in friendships too

i walked offstage
once the show was over
and prayed for the misery to
stop eating me alive
i was sick
and pretending not to be sick
at least performing kept me moving
coming home to an
empty apartment was worse
without work i had nothing to look forward to
i'd sink into the depression for months
half passed out from the grief
eyes open
mind lost in another dimension
write the book they said
get back on the road again
what's taking you so long

- *empty*

i want to live
i'm just afraid
i won't measure up to the
idea people have of me in their heads
i'm afraid of getting older
scared i'll never write anything
worth reading again
that i'll disappoint the people
who are counting on me
that i'll never learn how to be happy
that i'll be broke again one day
that my parents will die
and i'll be alone in the end

being molested as a child has been the most confusing
experience of my life. to learn sex without having any
concept of it has messed me up in more ways than
i'm aware of. to feel an orgasm so young. to have my
life threatened. to be stretched. bruised. bit. spit on.
to become a woman at the age of four. to know fear
intimately. have it breathe down my neck. to be numb.
stiff. silent. and own all the world's shame at once.

the need to survive
lit a fire in me

i want to be snapped
cracked
hammered into
i want to open where i am closed
find the secret door
let me out of me
i want something to
hold me by the neck
split me down the middle
and make me feel alive again

- *i don't want to be numb anymore*

i am trusting the uncertainty
and believing i will
end up somewhere
right and good

there is nothing wrong with you
this is growth
this is transformation
protecting yourself
getting lost in the noise
figuring it out
feeling used
uncared for
losing hope
burning out
this is fear
this is processing
this is surviving
this is being alive

- journey

you lose everything
when you don't love yourself

- *and gain everything when you do*

i am not my worst days
i am not what happened to me

- *reminder*

there are whole blackouts
in some of the years i have lived
my therapist says our minds erase trauma
to help us move on
but every experience i've had
is memorized in my flesh
even if my mind forgets
my body remembers
my body is the map of my life
my body wears what it's been through
my body signals the alarms when
it thinks danger is coming
and suddenly
the hungry little demons from my past
come raging out of my flesh
screaming
don't you forget us
don't you ever try to
leave us behind again

i'm either romanticizing the past
or i'm busy worrying about the future
it's no wonder
i don't feel alive
i'm not living
in the only moment that's real

- *present*

anxiety feels like i'm hanging
off the side of a building
and my hand is going to
slip any second

how can i be so
cruel to myself
when i'm doing the best i can

- *be gentle*

list of things to heal your mood:

1) cry it. walk it. write it. scream it. dance it
   out of your body.
2) if after all that
   you are still
   spiraling out of control
   ask yourself if sinking into the mud is worth it
3) the answer is no
4) the answer is breathe
5) sip tea and feel your nervous system settle
6) you are the hero of your life
7) this feeling doesn't have power over you
8) the universe has prepared you to handle this
9) no matter how dark it gets
   the light is always on its way
10) you are the light
11) walk yourself back to where the love lives

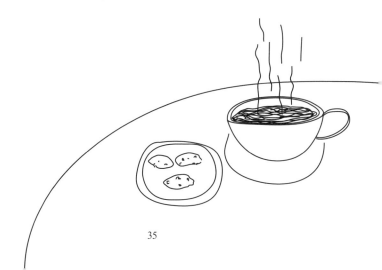

i am not broken
because of the depression
i am not a lesser version of myself
because of the anxiety
i am a whole
complete
and complicated person

- full

i am loving myself out of the dark

i'm breathing aren't i
that's gotta be a sign that
the universe is on my side
if i've made it this far
i can make it all the way

imagine what we could accomplish if
we didn't have to spend our energy
protecting ourselves from
society's rapist problem

most of my life has been spent
with the two of us touching
skin to skin
our nights together
and sometimes our days
you carried me when my limbs refused to
when i was so sick i could not move
not once did you tire of my weight
not once did you complain
you've witnessed all my dreams
my sex
my writing
my weeping
every vulnerable act of my life
has been with you
the two of us knee-deep in laughter
and when i've been a fool to trust a fool
made love on top of you
left for days only to
return empty-handed
you always took me back
when sleep abandoned me
we lay awake together
you are the embrace of my life
my confessional
my altar
i went from girl to woman on top of you
and in the end
it will be you—old friend
delivering me to death well rested

- *there is no place more intimate than a bed*

you didn't lose it
happiness has always been here

- *you just lost perspective*

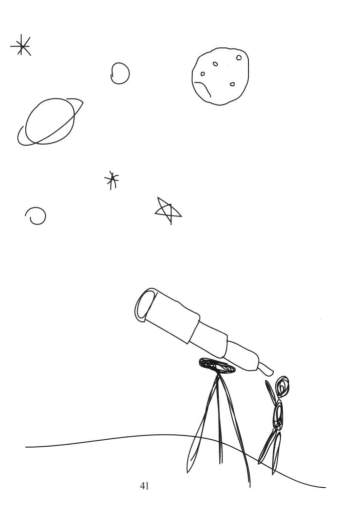

what we lived through
is living in us

i am not a victim of my life
what i went through
pulled a warrior out of me
and it is my greatest honor to be her

for the love of my life
i am trying my best to have hope
i'll keep greeting each morning
with an *i will*
when it feels like i can't
i will
i will
i will
meet a day that will melt me
i will move and the sadness *will*
fall off my shoulders
to make room for joy
i will be full of color
i will touch the sky again

i want a parade
i want music
i want confetti
i want a marching band
for the ones surviving in silence
i want a standing ovation
for every person who
wakes up and moves toward the sun
when there is a shadow
pulling them back on the inside

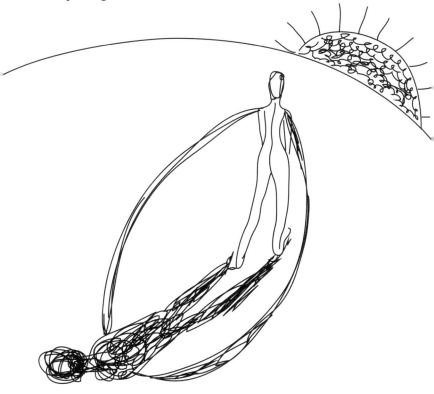

our pain is the doorway to our joy

i'm tired of being disappointed
in the home that keeps me alive
i'm exhausted by the energy it takes
to hate myself

- *i'm putting the hate down*

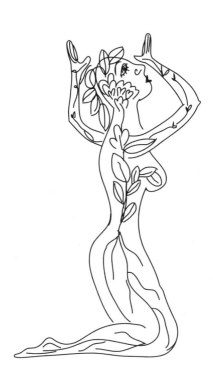

heart

sometimes
i love you means
i want to love you

sometimes
i love you means
i'll stay a little while longer

sometimes
i love you means
i'm not sure how to leave

sometimes
i love you means
i have nowhere else to go

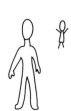

i have difficulty separating
abusive relationships
from healthy ones
i can't tell the difference
between love and violence

- *it all looks the same*

i was trying to make him the one
and it took me three years to realize
love doesn't work like that

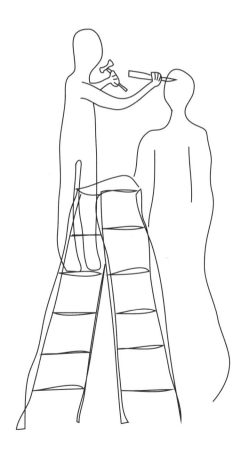

men like him are experts at
smelling out girls like me
the invisible ones
who believe they must be ugly
because their fathers didn't love them
he said my name
and i had never heard my name
dance off a man's lips before
give a little attention
to someone who's never had any
and they'll be slipping and falling
all over the place
unable to contain the joy
of being wanted
the relief of being discovered
he groomed me into thinking
i couldn't survive without him
this is how men like him
trap girls like me

- predator

don't ask me why i didn't leave
he made my world so small
i couldn't see the exit

- i'm surprised i got out at all

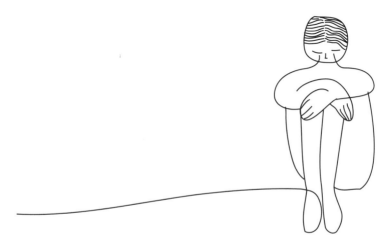

if someone doesn't have a heart
you can't go around
offering them yours

each time i showed you a piece of heaven
it was a warning
every stroll we took
through the garden of my life
all the flowers that bloomed for you
the peacocks that sang your name
were a sign
yet
after seeing all my magic
you hit your head and lost it
went and scattered yourself across this town
thinking if you were lucky enough to taste me
you'd get your hands on something better
everything dulled in comparison
now you're back
body spilling all over my floor
begging me
to crush you with my thighs
pull you into my hips
transcend you to heaven with my pussy
i had you on the greatest trip of your life
i had you seeing visions
each time i showed you a piece of heaven
every stroll we took through the garden of my life
all the flowers that bloomed for you
the peacocks that sang your name
were a sign of all you'd lose
if you betrayed me

- *consequences*

if you're waiting for them
to make you feel like you're enough
you'll be waiting a long time

i'm leaving
cause i'm not happy here
i don't want to reach the end of my life
still having doubts about
the man i've been with
since my twenties

why does everything
become less beautiful
once it belongs to us

it took me getting into a healthy relationship
to realize i shouldn't be scared
of the person i love

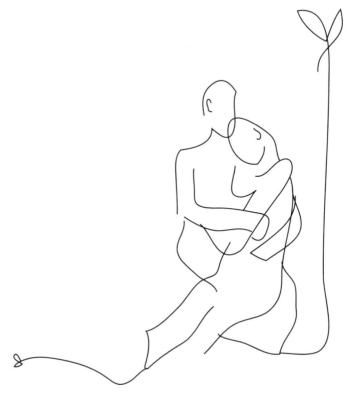

i used to cry
because i could not find
a good man to love me
now i have one and
he isn't enough
the others were always
halfway out the door

- that's what made them alluring

why do i hurt the ones
who want to lift me up and
worship the ones who crush me

- *what made me like this*

i don't know what to do with a man
who wants to hold on to me
for the rest of our lives

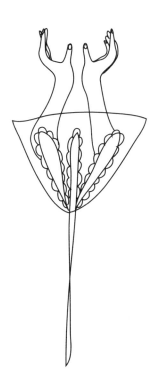

i'm afraid i won't find the one who sees me
and rushes to breathe me in
i have a fear of seeming too desperate
i'm scared i will be cheated on
with a woman more brilliant
more striking
more of me in every way
terrified this will confirm what i know already
that i am not enough for someone to stay
where is the burning match that will set me on fire
what if i've already walked by the one
on a street corner
what if i've already been with them
and ruined it
who will love me enough to
spend their energy getting close
to someone so inconsistent
what if the one i want
is someone who touches me and leaves
and the one who doesn't leave
is someone i can't stand touching me
will it always be bad timing
will i ever be sure
will i settle
will i be on my own forever

your partner is supposed to
enrich your life
not drain it
staying when it hurts is not love

i'm too in love with my life
to be spilling all over the floor
for the next man
who gives me butterflies
when i could look in the mirror
and take my own breath away

the love of family
friends and community
is just as potent
as the love
of a romantic relationship

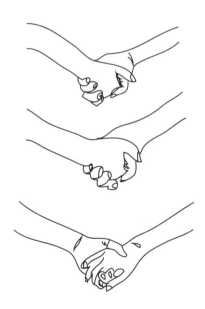

nothing can replace
how the women in my life
make me feel

it's impossible
for one person to
fill you up
in all the ways
you need to be filled
your partner
can't be your everything

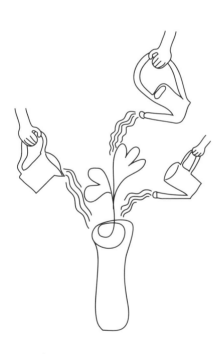

i can live without romantic love
but i can't survive without
the women i call friends
they know exactly what i need
before i even know i need it
the way we hold space
for each other is just different

a man can't give me anything
i can't give myself

- *things i wish i could tell the younger me*

masturbation
is meditation

in a world that doesn't consider
my body to be mine
self-pleasure is an act
of self-preservation
when i'm feeling disconnected
i connect with my center
touch by touch
i drop back into myself
at the orgasm

i'm not going to pretend
to be less intelligent than i am
so a man can feel
more comfortable around me
the one i deserve
will see my greatness and
want to lift it higher

i want you to wipe away
everything you know about love
and start with one word
kindness
give it to them
let them give it to you
be two pillars
equal in your love
and you'll carry empires on your backs

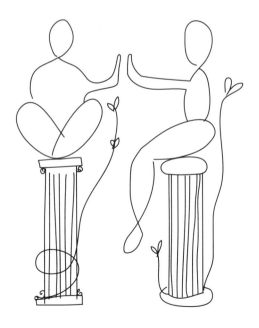

i wrap my holy legs
around his heavy head
and let his tongue swim
toward salvation

- *baptize*

i want someone who is
inspired by my brilliance
not threatened by it

look me in the eyes
when you're down there
eating for your life

- *i want you to see what you do to me*

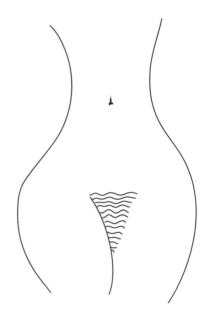

i'm careful about
who i spend my energy on

- *i know my worth*

my body is so hot from wanting you
i'm spilling by the time we take our clothes off
i want the kind of love that
transcends me
into another realm
i want you so deep
we enter the spirit world
go from being gentle to rough
i want eye contact
spread my legs to
opposite ends of the room
and look with your fingers
i want my soul to be touched
by the tip of yours
i want to come
out of this room
different people

- can you do that

rest

there are years in me
that have not slept

i measure my self-worth
by how productive i've been
but no matter
how hard i work
i still feel inadequate

- *productivity guilt*

i fear that
my best years are behind me
and nothing beyond this point will add up

productivity

anxiety

i have this productivity anxiety
that everyone else is working harder than me
and i'm going to be left behind
cause i'm not working fast enough
long enough
and i'm wasting my time

i don't sit down to have breakfast
i take it to go
i call my mother when i'm free—otherwise
it takes too long to have a conversation

i put off everything that
won't bring me closer to my dreams
as if the things i'm putting off
are not the dream themselves

isn't the dream
that i have a mother to call
and a table to eat breakfast at

instead i'm lost in the sick need
to optimize every hour of my day
so i'm improving in some way
making money in some way
advancing my career in some way
because that's what it takes
to be successful
right

i excavate my life
package it up
sell it to the world
and when they ask for more
i dig through bones
trying to write poems

capitalism got inside my head
and made me think my only value
is how much i produce
for people to consume
capitalism got inside my head
and made me think
i am of worth
as long as i am working

i learned impatience from it
i learned self-doubt from it
learned to plant seeds in the ground
and expect flowers the next day

but magic
doesn't work like that
magic doesn't happen
cause i've figured out how to
pack more work in a day
magic moves
by the laws of nature
and nature has its own clock
magic happens
when we play
when we escape
daydream and imagine
that's where everything
with the power to fulfill us
is waiting on its knees for us

- *productivity anxiety*

we can work
at our own pace
and still be
successful

a

lifetime

on the road

while i was growing up
my dad worked six days a week
driving an eighteen-wheeler truck
from one end of the continent to the other

he'd come home
after a week on the road
while my siblings and i would be sleeping
the sound of the front door always woke me
the basement we lived in was small
i could hear mom in the kitchen
making him a fresh meal of dal and roti

dad would eat
shower
settle into bed
but as soon as his eyes drifted off
his boss would call and say

get back on the road again
and just like that
we'd catch a glimpse of dad leaving

when you're an immigrant
you keep your head down and stay working
when you're a refugee and
you don't have papers
when they call you illegal
outsider
terrorist
towelhead
you work until your bones become dust
you are the only one you can count on

every time he started at a new company
he'd spend months working for free
during their mandatory "training" period
funny how they needed to train a man
who was fully licensed
qualified
and experienced

after the third month of
not taking a penny home
dad would demand compensation
and they'd offer him
five cents for every mile he drove

years ago while driving a load
from montreal to florida
he ended up at a hospital

somewhere in the middle of america
with his appendix moments away
from bursting

when the doctor told him
they had to get him into surgery immediately
he looked at her and said
i can't afford it
can this wait until i get back home to canada

when do you get back home the doctor asked

in three days he responded
and she looked at him like he must
be out of his mind

luckily
she didn't have it in her
to let him risk his life
she performed the surgery for free that night
and you want to know what my dad did
right after they stitched him up
he walked out of the hospital
climbed into his truck
finished the delivery
and spent three days driving back home

why would you put yourself through that i ask
he shrugs his shoulders and tells me
my boss wouldn't get me a flight home
where would i leave my truck

i couldn't drive back with a trailer full
of undelivered car parts
and risk losing my job

while listening to him
all i can think is that
no one should have to work to the bone like that
it breaks me into pieces to hear
about every person who grinds
for less than what they're worth
how do we sleep at night
knowing the systems we uphold
treat the foundations of our society
as second-class citizens
when they are the reason
the wheels of this world stay turning

i want to give my dad
a lifetime of peace
for the lifetime he spent
on the road to feed us
i want him to know
what comfort feels like
i want him to see
he's done enough

- *a lifetime on the road*

when the kids at school asked
where my mom worked
i lied and said *at the factory*
like all the other moms
i was too embarrassed to admit
she didn't have a "real job"
even though "stay-at-home mom" meant
she was a full-time caregiver
driver
chef
secretary
tutor
cleaner
best friend
of four kids and
the world's definition of a "real job"
couldn't begin to cover all that

- *value*

we were always in survival mode
long after we didn't need to be

- *habit*

i'm stuck in
this constant cycle
of running off to build my life
and running back cause
i feel guilty about not
spending enough time with them

- *parent-guilt*

i thought my brown immigrant body
should always work harder
than everyone else in the room
because that's what made me valuable

our elders are not disposable

the land sprawled its limbs
and said *put your feet up*
the trees said *we will give you life*
the air said *breathe me in*
the earth said
take care of what takes care of you
and we turned our backs on all of them

- betrayal

we've ruined
our only home for
convenience and profit
neither of which will be
useful once the earth
can't breathe

being the loudest on earth's playground
doesn't make us any more important than
the dirt we crush beneath our feet
we are nothing except air
and fire and water and soil
we are a people
who forget what we are made of
a people who talk about the weather
as if it's mundane and not magic
as if the oceans
are not holy water
as if the sky
is not a vision
as if the animals
are not our siblings
as if nature is not god
and rain is not god's tears
and we are not god's children
as if god is not the earth itself

i was trying to fit into a system
that left me empty

- *capitalism*

i thought i could
accomplish my way
into being happy
but nothing on the outside
fulfilled me in the ways
it had promised

happiness grew old
waiting for me
and i grew old
searching for happiness
in places it did not live

our souls
will not be soothed
by what we achieve
how we look
or all the hard work we do
even if we managed to
make all the money in the world
we'd be left feeling empty for something
our souls ache for community
our deepest being craves one another
we need to be connected
to feel alive

i get so lost
in where i want to go
i forget that the place i'm in
is already quite magical

i miss the days my friends
knew every mundane detail about my life
and i knew every ordinary detail about theirs
adulthood has starved me of that consistency
that *us*
the walks around the block
the long conversations when we were
too lost in the moment to care what time it was
when we won and celebrated
when we failed and celebrated harder
when we were *just kids*
now we have our very important jobs
that fill up our very busy schedules
we compare calendars just to plan coffee dates
that one of us eventually cancels
cause adulthood is being too exhausted
to leave our apartments most days
i miss knowing i once belonged
to a group of people bigger than myself
that belonging made life easier to live

- *friendship nostalgia*

we already have the things that can complete us
they just aren't things
they are people
and laughter and connection

- *irreplaceable*

you might have done
the external work
but your mind is starving
for internal attention

- listen

i'm throwing the whole concept of
commercialized self-help out altogether
i'm tired of buying products and services
that don't make me feel any better

- *empty promises*

i don't care about perfection
i'd rather roll deep
in the messiness of life

we think we are lost
while our fuller
found and complete selves
are somewhere in the future
we get on our hands and knees
thinking self-improvement will
help us reach them
but this finding ourselves bullshit
is never going to end
i'm tired of putting off living until
i have more information on who i am
i'm a new person every month
always becoming and unbecoming
only to become again
our fuller selves are not off in the future
they're right here
in the only moment that exists
i don't need fixing
i will be searching for answers my whole life
not because i'm a half-formed thing
but because i'm brilliant enough to keep growing
everything necessary to live a vivid life
already exists in me

- *i am complete simply because i am imperfect*

productivity is not how much
work i do in a day
but how well i balance
what i need to stay healthy

- being productive is knowing when to rest

i have to honor my mind and body
if i want to sustain this journey

- *life*

no one is qualified to decide your worth
you wake up and live your life every day
yours is the only opinion of you
that matters

little poet
it seems like the more words you write
the more you think
it is you writing them
why do you think you're in control
didn't the words come spilling
out of you the first time
pouring without permission
and now you're trying to
make them work for you
but magic doesn't move like that
your rushing is
suffocating the masterpieces
baking inside you
your job is to
show up for the process
be patient and when it's time
the universe will use you again

- inspiration

if you tried
and didn't end up
where you wanted to go
that's still progress

quiet down i begged my mind
your overthinking is
robbing us of joy

not everything you do has
to be self-improving
you are not a machine
you are a person
without rest
your work can never be full
without play
your mind can never be nourished

- *balance*

play is when we escape time

if you want to be creative
you need to learn how to
do stuff that has no purpose
art isn't made by
working all the time
first you've got to
go out and live

- the art will come

get out of your own way
get out of your own way
get out of your own way

i'm done trying to
prove myself
to myself

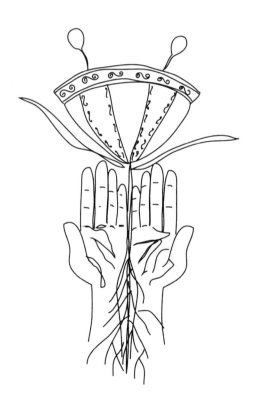

i became confident
once i decided that having fun
was far more important than
my fear of looking silly

- *dancing in public*

we've worked so hard
to be here
we can afford to
slow down and enjoy the view

awake

i'm waking up
from the longest night of my life
it's been years since i've seen the sun

- *awakening*

you can't quiet a woman who was born muzzled

i fell from the mouth of my mother's legs
into the palms of this world
with god herself raging in me

- *birth*

i paid in blood to be here. i paid with a childhood littered with bigger monsters than you. i've been beaten into a silence more times than i've been embraced on this earth. you haven't seen what i've seen. my rock bottom went so deep i'm pretty sure it was hell. i spent a decade climbing out of it. my hands blistered. my feet swelled. my mind said *i can't take it anymore.* i told my mind *you better get yourself together. we came here for joy. and we are going to feel all of it.* i've been hunted. killed. and walked back to earth. i snapped the neck off every beast that thought it could. and you want to take my seat. the one i built with the story of my life. honey. you won't fit. i juggle clowns like you. i pick my teeth with fools like you for fun. i have played and slept and danced with bigger devils.

on days you can't hear yourself
slow down to
let your mind and body
catch up to each other

- *stillness*

what a relief
to discover that
the aches i thought
were mine alone
are also felt by
so many others

my body renews itself in waves of ocean and blood

i have a very complicated relationship
with the country i was born in
our men were
slaughtered in those streets
our women were raped
while thousands were tortured
and disappeared by police
the indian state denies what they did
but no amount of yoga or bollywood
can make us forget the
sikh genocide they orchestrated

- never forget 1984

i will never be quiet
about the way my
people resisted
so i could be free

our wounds are the reason
i started writing poetry
every word
i've ever written was to
lead us back into our arms

they could take away
everything we have
and we'd conjure this
beautiful life up all over again
with the bones in our backs
building an empire
from the ground up
is exactly what we're good at

ours must be
a politic of revolution
freedom can't exist
until the most disadvantaged are free

don't sleep on
the doormat of your potential
waiting for things to happen
when you could *be*
the thing that happens

you are one person
but when you move
an entire community
walks through you

- you go nowhere alone

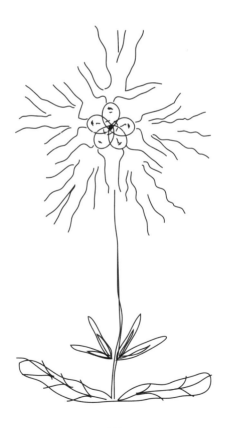

by virtue of living
in a racist world
nonblack people are
raised to be antiblack
we are all taught that
lighter is better

- *undoing*

your voice
is your sovereignty

- *free*

you look tired he says
i turn to him and say
yeah i'm exhausted
i've been fighting misogyny for decades
how else do you expect me to look

no one on this planet
is in more denial
than the white man
who regardless of all
the evidence in front of him
still thinks racism and sexism
and all the world's pain don't exist

the world is changing
can you feel it
undressing itself and slipping into
something uncomfortable
and more just

- *waves*

i'm not interested
in a feminism that thinks
simply placing women at the top
of oppressive systems is progress

- *not your convenient figurehead*

the future
world of our dreams
can't be built on the
corruptions of the past

- tear it down

today i saw myself for the first time
when i dusted off
the mirror of my mind
and the woman looking back
took my breath away
who was this beautiful beastling
this extra-celestial earthling
i touched my face and my reflection
touched the woman of my dreams
all her gorgeous smirking back at me
my knees surrendered to the earth
as i wept and sighed at how
i'd gone my whole life
being myself
but not seeing myself
spent decades living inside my body
never left it once
yet managed to miss all its miracles
isn't it funny how you can
occupy a space without
being in touch with it
how it took so long for me
to open the eyes of my eyes
embrace the heart of my heart
kiss the soles of my swollen feet
and hear them whisper
thank you
thank you
thank you
for noticing

you have everything to gain
from believing in yourself
yet you spend all your time with self-doubt

there is a conversation
happening inside you
pay deep attention
to what your inner world
is saying

i stopped resisting
the unpleasant feelings
and accepted that happiness
has nothing to do with
feeling good all the time

- *balance*

it's easy to love
the nice things about ourselves
but true self-love is
embracing the difficult parts
that live in all of us

- *acceptance*

can you hear the women who came before me
five hundred thousand voices
ringing through my neck
as if this were all a stage built for them
i can't tell which parts of me are me
and which parts are them
can you see them taking over my spirit
shaking out of my limbs
to do everything
they couldn't do
when they were alive

i dive into the well of my body
and end up in another world
everything i need
already exists in me
there's no need
to look anywhere else

- *home*

oh but the pussy is brave
lest we forget
how much pain
the pussy can take
how much pleasure it delivers
unto itself and others
remember
how it spit you out
without a flinch
now here you are
using the word *pussy*
like an insult
when you're not even
strong enough to be one

live loud and proud like you deserve
and reject their bullshit definition
of what a woman should look like

women have been starved of space for so long
when one of us finally
makes it into the arena
we get scared that another woman
will take our spot
but space doesn't work like that
look at all the men in the arena getting stronger
as their numbers multiply
more women in the arena means
more room for all of us to rise

- *stronger together*

i am not interested in a feminism
that excludes trans women

he says *you're opinionated*
as if it's an insult
to have ideas so big
he chokes on the size of them

- *never be quiet*

look for the women in the room
who have less space than you
listen
hear them
and act on what they're saying

- *amplify indigenous. trans. black. brown.*
  women of color voices.

why escape yourself
when you are so beautiful
get closer to your shine

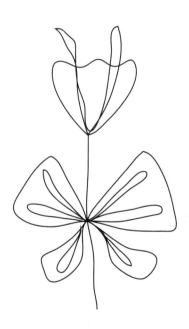

on days i could not move
it was women
who came to water my feet
until i was strong enough
to stand
it was women
who nourished me
back to life

- *sisters*

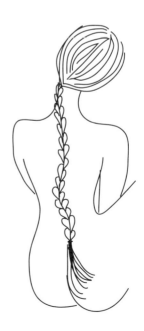

make it a point
to love yourself
as fiercely as you do other people

- *commitment*

it shouldn't affect anyone
what we do with our bodies
least of all those who haven't
walked a day in our shoes

give me laugh lines and wrinkles
i want proof of the jokes we shared
engrave the lines into my face like
the roots of a tree that grow deeper
with each passing year
i want sunspots as souvenirs
for the beaches we laid on
i want to look like i was
never afraid to let the world
take me by the hand
and show me what it's made of
i want to leave this place knowing
i did something with my body
other than trying to
make it look perfect

i can't take my eyes off of me
now that i see myself
i can't take my mind off of me
can't believe the tricks
my hands have been up to
the sermons i spoke into existence
the mountains i crushed
with my fingers
and the mountains i built
from all the shit
people tried to
stone me to death with

- warrior

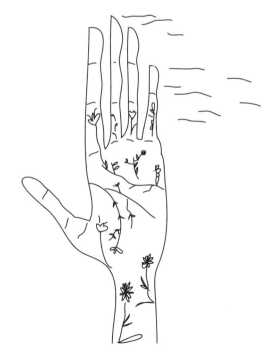

i often daydream about the woman i'll be
when i leave the rush of
my insecure twenties
and pick up self-assurance on the way
i can't wait to make
my eighteen-year-old self jealous
of the hell i raise
roaring into my thirties and forties
my soul becoming
more potent with age
at fifty i'll sit with
my wrinkles and silver hair
laughing about the adventures
we've had together
talking about the countless more
in the decades ahead
what a privilege it is
to grow into the
finest version of myself

- *aging*

be here
in what needs to be done today

- *that's how you honor tomorrow*

if the devil hadn't
pushed you into a corner
and forced you to break its neck
how would you have known
you were this strong

there are miracles in me
waiting their turn to happen
i am never giving up on myself

you do not belong to the future or the past

- *you belong right here*

get loud
say what you need to say
it feels good to reclaim your life

the way we rise
from every sorrow in life
is the most gorgeous thing i've seen

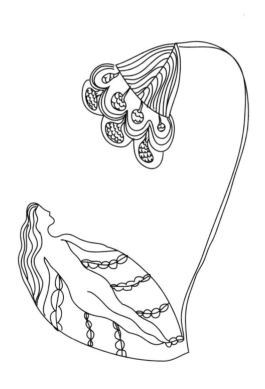

you are a soul. a world. a portal. a spirit. you are never alone. you are organs and blood and flesh and muscle. a colony of miracles weaving into each other.

break down
every door they built
to keep you out
and bring all your people with you

- *storm*

you are not alone
alone would be if
your heart no longer beat
and your lungs no longer pulled
and your breath no longer pushed
how are you alone if
an entire community lives in you

- you have all of you on your side

i will never have
this version of me again
let me slow down
and be with her

- always evolving

your beauty is undeniable
but everything sacred and ancient in you
is even more stunning

i am waking up to my godself

nothing tastes better than
being on your own side

i'm not afraid of failing
i'm afraid my potential
might set the world on fire

there are days
when the light flickers
and then i remember
i am the light
i go in and
switch it back on

- *power*

you have only scratched the surface
of what you're capable of
there are decades
of victories ahead of you

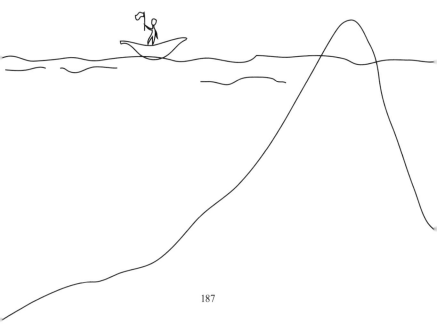

silly girl
little angel
little devil
so oblivious to
being the miracle worker
you are the mother
the magician
the master of your life

now that you are free
and the only obligation you are under
is your own dreams
what will you do
with your time

poems
illustrations
and cover art by:

rupi kaur

other books by rupi kaur:

milk and honey
the sun and her flowers

Rupi Kaur is a poet, artist, and performer.

A breakout literary phenomenon and #1 *New York Times* bestselling author, Rupi Kaur wrote, illustrated, and self-published her first poetry collection, *milk and honey* (2014). Next came its artistic siblings, *the sun and her flowers* (2017) and *home body* (2020), both debuting at #1 on bestseller lists across the world. These collections have sold over 11 million copies and have been translated into over 43 languages, with *milk and honey* surpassing Homer's *Odyssey* as the bestselling poetry of all time. She was also regarded as "writer of the decade" by the *New Republic* and recognized on the *Forbes* 30 under 30 list. In 2022, Kaur released her fourth book, *Healing Through Words*, another bestseller and a journey of guided writing exercises to help readers explore their creativity.

As she has done from the very beginning, Kaur self-produced *Rupi Kaur Live* (2021), the first-of-its-kind poetry special on Amazon Prime Video. Kaur also wrote and narrated an original poem for the short film *Rise* with Reese Witherspoon's media company Hello Sunshine. *Rise* was showcased at the 2023 Sundance Film Festival and is now available on Amazon Prime Video.

Kaur has also graced stages across the globe and completed another sold-out tour in 2023. Her shows are poetic theatrical experiences interlaced with Kaur's own touch of stand-up.

Kaur's work encompasses love, loss, trauma, healing, femininity, and migration. She feels most at home when creating art, performing her poetry onstage, and spending time with family and friends.

Andrews McMeel Publishing
a division of Andrews McMeel Universal
1130 Walnut Street, Kansas City, Missouri 64106

www.andrewsmcmeel.com
www.rupikaur.com

24 25 26 27 28 SDB 10 9 8 7 6 5

ISBN: 978-1-4494-8680-8

Library of Congress Control Number: 2020945169

Illustrations and cover design by Rupi Kaur

MIX
Paper | Supporting
responsible forestry
FSC® C144853

ATTENTION: SCHOOLS AND BUSINESSES
Andrews McMeel books are available at quantity discounts with bulk purchase
for educational, business, or sales promotional use. For information, please
e-mail the Andrews McMeel Publishing Special Sales Department:
sales@amuniversal.com.